West Lake Reflections

—A Guide to Hangzhou

Sara Grimes

PEOPLE'S PUBLISHING HOUSE ZHEJIANG
FOREIGN LANGUAGES PRESS BEIJING

First Edition   1983

ISBN   0-8351-1012-5

Published by the People's Publishing House, Zhejiang Province
and the Foreign Languages Press
24 Baiwanzhuang Road, Beijing, China

Printed by the Foreign Languages Printing House
19 West Chegongzhuang Road, Beijing, China

Distributed by China Publications Center (Guoji Shudian)
P.O. Box 399, Beijing, China

Printed in the People's Republic of China

Contents

Preface

We were in a boat gliding along in a mist on the West Lake when I remarked to one of my Hangzhou colleagues that during an early morning walk along the lake I had been struck by the beauty of Xiling Bridge as its graceful lines emerged from and contrasted with the grey of the fog.

"Ah yes," he replied, "this is what Su Dongpo meant when he compared the West Lake to the famous ancient beauty, Xi Zi. The West Lake always looks beautiful, in all weather."

Huang Youyi, also from the editorial staff of the Foreign Languages Press in Beijing, translated this for me while we both took notes on the allusion made by our colleague Sun Jiasui, an editor with the Committee for the Compilation of the Great Chinese Dictionary, to his favorite Northern Song Dynasty poet Su Dongpo. Soon afterwards, our host for the entire trip, He Qi, the editor in charge of all travel books with the People's Publishing House, Zhejiang Province, put in that a fairly large number of the boat drivers on the West Lake were — as was our driver — women.

This was how it went for ten days in Hangzhou — three Chinese and an American working together to try to produce a book that reflects today's Hangzhou along with its history in a way that is meaningful to Western readers.

Comparing the West Lake to Xi Zi may have meaning

for Chinese (although the older generation in China might complain that there is some doubt about that among the younger generation), but how to make a comparison that Westerners can understand?

Some similarities exist between Hangzhou and its official sister city in the United States, Boston. Both have religious sites of historic importance (Temple of the Soul's Retreat, also known as Lingyin Temple, and Old Christ Church), are state capitals (Zhejiang Province and Massachusetts), and have shrines to patriotic figures (Yue Fei's Temple and Paul Revere's homestead), legendary tales surrounding historic events (Emperor Kangxi at the Temple of the Soul's Retreat and the Boston Tea Party), major literary figures (to mention only two for both cities: Su Dongpo and Bai Juyi; Emerson and Thoreau), numerous institutes of higher learning, a treasured fresh body of water (the West Lake and the Charles River) and excellent fish restaurants.

A fundamental difference is that while Boston's attractions are an integral part of the city — the scenic, cultural and historic attractions of Hangzhou are for the most part on its outskirts.

As our boat reached the Mid-Lake Pavilion, I discovered my camera was missing. By the time we left the island some ten minutes later, the camera had reappeared — compliments of a leisure boat driver to whom it had been given for delivery to me by the driver of the taxi in which I'd left it.

Such courtesy and friendliness characterized our contact with people in Hangzhou — from the little boys playing around the massive rocks near Baochu Pagoda who stopped to have their picture taken with us, to the truck drivers on holiday from a nearby city who shared a beer and conversation at the Yue Fei Lake Tower Restaurant, to the workers and supervisors on whom we dropped in unannounced at major scenic sites and to the formal interviews over tea granted us by representatives of the silk and tourist industries and the Hangzhou Parks Administration.

Sometimes we surprised each other: I was surprised to learn in our interview with the silk industry people that one-third of all silk distributed domestically goes to the minority autonomous regions of Inner Mongolia and Tibet. They were surprised to learn from me that most American women, in my opinion, do not own a silk blouse. I recommended to them that China's silk industry get away from the floral patterns for export which we think old-fashioned and search our fashion magazines for more modern prints. They assured me they are working on this — and indications are that they are. Hangzhou silk offers some of the most contemporary patterns available in China. (Although I happened to have had one silk blouse before coming to China, I have become addicted to them here in less than a year and now own several.)

Luck also seemed to follow us. On the CAAC flight from Beijing to Hangzhou, Huang Youyi and I by chance sat next to Bao Defa, a cadre of the Urban Division of the Hangzhou Parks Administration, who became our first interview.

"I helped plant trees with Nixon," he said, referring to former U.S. President Richard M. Nixon's trip to Hangzhou on his 1972 visit which opened the way towards normalization of relations between the People's Republic of China and the United States. Bao was on his way back from the capital where he'd gone to get a visa for travel to Hongkong where he'd been invited to help plan

3

a West Lake lantern festival in one of that city's parks.

"I've been to many places but there's none better than Hangzhou. There's nowhere the air is as fresh," said Bao.

Having worked for the Hangzhou Parks Administration since the 1960s, Bao witnessed the "cultural revolution" — the most recent period of many in history in which Hangzhou suffered destruction under internal turmoil or foreign intervention.

"It's a hard story to tell. Gardeners couldn't work because they would be criticized for trying to bring back feudal things. But that's not the worst. The worst was the destruction of things that can't be brought back. At that time I worked in the southern district where there are three caves with stone carvings. The bottom cave with 500 Buddhas was completely destroyed. I saw some people come and smash the noses, eyes and mouths of the statues with their hammers. This is something that can't be brought back. There's no point in rebuilding 500 Buddhas — the special thing about them was that they were ancient. We all felt very sad."

A national treasure that did survive the "cultural revolution" practically unscathed — thanks greatly to the late Premier Zhou Enlai — was the Temple of the Soul's Retreat. As luck would have it, the day we visited the temple happened to coincide with a visit by Yu Yongxi, Secretary-General of the Hangzhou Buddhist Society, a member of the Tiantai Sect of Buddhism who talked with us for nearly an hour about the history of the temple in an impromptu interview over tea in the reception room next to the temple's vegetarian restaurant.

At this point, our Hangzhou colleagues He Qi and Sun Jiasui began to take note of our luck and read auspicious signs in the names of the next two people we interviewed:

4

Li Xinbing (Li the New Soldier), a saleswoman at the Xiling Seal-Engraving Society who told us about the new interest in China in traditional chops and Chen Tugen (Chen Root-Earth), the gardener at the Hangzhou Flower Nursery who gave us a detailed account of the fine art of raising bonsai.

At the vast Hangzhou Botanical Gardens, it was our good fortune to run into Tang Hairong, supervisor of the herb garden, who took time from his lunch break to take us on an extensive tour.

And the best sign of all — on the last day of our trip our driver for most of the ten days, Wang Rongrong, ended a month of struggle by solving the Rubik Cube.

Even the mid-January weather was unusual in that it gave me a good chance to see Hangzhou in almost every possible condition. It was 60 degrees (F) and bright and sunny when we arrived. Over the next days it was overcast, rainy, foggy, snowy, and bright and clear but cold. At each site under all these conditions, we paused at the entrance as He Qi and Sun Jiasui worked with Huang Youyi and me to get the right English translation of the Chinese calligraphy at the gate.

It was the coldest day of the year the day we visited the Meijiawu Tea Brigade, according to Chen Wuyun, the brigade leader. I was so fascinated by her account of her own life and tea production that I may have kept my colleagues waiting too long as we sat around a mahogany table sipping tea in the brigade's unheated reception room. I apologized later.

"That's all right," said Huang Youyi. "If you'd asked one more question, I would have killed you."

At 8 a.m. the day we visited the Six Harmonies Pagoda overlooking the Qiantang River, it was snowing a heavy thick snow mixed with rain. As we trudged up the stone steps under umbrellas to the pagoda — me in boots loaned to me by He Qi's wife — I asked Sun Jiasui for some appropriate lines of poetry to match the occasion.

"Today," he said in slow English and mock gravity, "I feel no inspiration."

But later he was inspired enough to help He Qi write a poem for me that He Qi read at a farewell banquet given by the People's Publishing House, Zhejiang Province at the Hangzhou Restaurant:

> Green hills and clear waters embrace you,
> And there falls a welcoming snow.
> Why is the West Lake scenery more beautiful than
>   ever?
> For it has been visited by an American admirer.

I want to thank my colleagues for their poem and for their great good humor and company throughout our working days and nights in Hangzhou and for their many contributions to this book. I'm sure they join me in thanking the people of Hangzhou — and finally, it's the people any place that really make it interesting — for their warm and gracious welcome.

Sara Grimes
August 5, 1982

Introduction

Hangzhou's reputation for scenic beauty — enhanced by its history as a Southern Song Dynasty capital and its long association with tea production and silk industry — has made Hangzhou with its West Lake a major cultural and resort city in southeast China for centuries.

Hangzhou attractions have given rise to legends, inspired poems and even generated a popular expression which goes so far as to say: "In heaven there is paradise, on earth there are Suzhou and Hangzhou." A more critical appraisal is offered by Wang Pingyu, deputy chief engineer with 33 years of experience in the Hangzhou Parks Administration, the agency which manages most of Hangzhou's historic and scenic sites.

"It's not enough to mention each site at Hangzhou," said Wang. "It's the overall view that must be shown to catch its character — its long history, the river, the lake, and the hills."

Part of the overall view is the size of Hangzhou — with its 57 scenic spots spread over 49 square kilometers of low hills and flatlands near the Qiantang River. This distinguishes it from the equally famous Suzhou, in the south of Jiangsu Province, with its individual gardens, and from Guilin, in the Guangxi Zhuang Autonomous Region, which has one dimension stretching along the Lijiang River.

Another characteristic of Hangzhou is the subtle proportions at West Lake created by the hills, which are all under 412.5 meters, and the lake, which is 5.6 square kilometers in area. "So the hills are not rough, and the lake is gentle. This is a unique feature. It's not like Taihu Lake (near Suzhou) which is just gigantic," Wang said.

The third important Hangzhou characteristic is the close association between its scenic spots and legends and historical figures like Yue Fei, the Song Dynasty commander (1103-42); Bai Juyi, the Tang Dynasty poet (772-846); Su Dongpo, the Northern Song poet (1037-1101); and Qiu Jin, the revolutionary woman hero (1877-1907).

"In fact, Hangzhou has important historical figures from almost every era. This lends a special aura of being poetic to the area. Without this historical link, the West Lake would not give such a deep impression," Wang said.

The Hangzhou Parks Administration, which employs about 5,100 persons, works year-round to maintain the some 30 scenic spots open to the public with gardening, landscaping and renovation work which has included reforesting over 10,000 acres (about 4,000 hectares) of land since the Liberation in 1949. Basic drainage and dredging of the lake is also an on-going process.

"We follow three principles in our work: the first is that everything is centered on the West Lake, the second is the protection of the ancient relics, and the third is the building up of the area through reforestation. We intend to make the whole area a garden," Wang said.

Wang added that any new construction must conform to guidelines established to maintain Hangzhou's character: construction must not be too high or wide which would put it out of proportion with the lake; buildings must not be too close together which might spoil a view; buildings must not be too foreign in style out of keeping with the national character of the area; nor must they be too dark, out of keeping with the bright style of local traditional architecture.

In pre-Liberation days, many of Hangzhou's scenic spots were deserted, "carved up" by individual owners, and in poor condition, according to Wang.

Today only a few cents will admit anyone to any of the major historic and scenic spots in Hangzhou which also include teahouses serving tea and sweets and concessions selling local handicrafts. They include: Baochu Pagoda, Flower Harbor Park, Jade Emperor Hill, Jade Spring, Temple of the Soul's Retreat, Listening to Orioles Singing in the Willows, the Three Caves at Yanxia, Nine Creeks and Eighteen Gullies, Six Harmonies Pagoda, Three Pools Mirroring the Moon, Tiger Spring, Wu Hill, Xiling Seal-Engraving Society, Yellow Dragon Cave, Yue Fei's Tomb and Temple, and Sun Yat-sen Park.

Recent major constructions undertaken by the Parks Administration include the building of a 4.23-kilometer-long road to a temple which had previously been accessible only by foot on the top of the 239-meter-high Jade Emperor Hill in 1977-78 at a cost of 650,000 yuan and the 1979 renovation of Yue Fei's Tomb and Temple, which had been severely damaged during the "cultural revolution," at a cost of 400,000 yuan. With an ever-increasing budget —the 1981 bureau budget of six million yuan triples that of ten years ago — the Bureau is looking forward to not only maintaining but expanding current sites, like the Lotus in the Breeze at Crooked Courtyard, and to restoring many others — especially under the influx of more foreign tourists.

But, finally, there is West Lake and the changing aspects of its beauty which have impressed so many visitors since ancient times — seen at dawn at Early Sun Terrace on Geling Hill, at sunset from Lakeside Park, at night at Autumn Moon on Calm Lake Pavilion, from afar on Jade Emperor Hill, from close up at Three Pools Mirroring the Moon. It was experiences like these in all seasons and in all weather which led Tang Dynasty poet Bai Juyi to write:

"One cannot bear to leave Hangzhou,
Part of the reason — this lake."

History

Since the Great Yu — the founder of the first dynasty
of China, Xia (c. 2100-1600 B.C.) — is reputed to have
visited the area, Hangzhou obviously has an ancient history.
But it was the building of the Grand Canal in the Sui
Dynasty (A.D. 581-618) that really spurred Hangzhou's
growth into a major cultural, economic and political center which reached its height when Hangzhou served as the
capital of the Southern Song Dynasty (1127-1279) for 153
years. An area blessed with great natural beauty, Hangzhou has also suffered terribly from wars and conflicts
throughout the centuries which have brought about the
building and rebuilding of its major historic sites, such as
the Temple of the Soul's Retreat and Yue Fei's Tomb and
Temple. Visits to these and other beautifully maintained
sites in Hangzhou can give a sense of what Hangzhou's
history has been as well as testify to China's present com-
mitment to the continued development of Hangzhou as
the capital of Zhejiang Province and to the preservation
of the West Lake as a scenic and historic park to be enjoyed by all.

The following gives a chronology of Hangzhou history
under the dynasties — which are often used in China to
describe the place in history in which a certain person,
building or event belongs.

Xia (c. 22nd-16th century B.C.)

The Great Yu, king of Xia, the legendary first Chinese dynasty, is said to be buried at Shaoxing, not far from Hangzhou.

(The Temple of Great Yu and his tomb were built five kilometers outside Shaoxing, the former in the 6th century while the time of construction of the latter remains unknown. *Lu's Almanac*, a book written at the end of the Warring States Period (770-475 B.C.), records the burial of Great Yu at Shaoxing. Some buildings at the site date from the 18th century.

(As early as 3,500 years ago, there were people living in the Hangzhou area. Archaeological finds at Liangzhu, 18 kilometers northwest of Hangzhou, indicate a primitive tribal village whose members were mostly engaged in agriculture once prospered on this fertile plain during the Neolithic Age. Examples of the finds are stone axes, knives, sickles, spades and porcelainware of beautiful patterns and shapes made with fine workmanship.

(In the early 1950s, construction workers found at the site for the new Zhejiang University campus near Laohe Hill northwest of West Lake a large number of artifacts dating back to the Neolithic Age. The findings include over 500 pieces of stone and jade objects, over 1,000 kilograms of bits and pieces of porcelainware, constituting the most complete and rich findings of Neolithic Age ever unearthed in the province.)

Shang (c. 16th-11th century B.C.) and Western Zhou (11th century-771 B.C.)

(Bronzeware from this period is on display at the Zhejiang Museum in Hangzhou.)

Eastern Zhou (770-256 B.C.) and Spring and Autumn Period (770-476 B.C.)

The kingdoms of Wu and Yue contend for rule in the Hangzhou region with Yue emerging as the winner. (Bronze swords from this period are displayed at the Zhejiang Museum.)

Warring States Period (475-221 B.C.) and Qin (221-207 B.C.)

A county government, Qiantang County, is established in the Hangzhou area under the prefecture of Guiji, now Shaoxing. The state of Chu south of the Changjiang River grows stronger in this period, eventually defeating Yue and unifies large areas of south China. As a result, Hangzhou becomes a part of Chu. *Records of the Historian*, Volume VI, a classical work of history written during 104 B.C. to 91 B.C. states that the First Emperor of Qin, after defeating the rival states and unifying China, pays a visit to Qiantang, an ancient name for Hangzhou. (A stone stands at the base of Precious Stone Hill in Hangzhou where the First Emperor of Qin is said to have tied his boat's mooring rope on a visit there.)

Western Han (206 B.C.-A.D. 24) and Eastern Han (25-220)

Hangzhou grows to become a major county of Guiji Prefecture and serves as the headquarters of the prefecture's military and security agencies. (Mirrors produced at Shaoxing during the Eastern Han decorated with chariots and horses are on display at the Zhejiang Museum.)

Three Kingdoms (220-280), Western Jin (265-316) and Eastern Jin (317-420)

Hangzhou, still called Qiantang County, expands and becomes prosperous.

Southern and Northern Dynasties (420-589)

County administration changed to a prefecture, known as Qiantang Prefecture.

326 — Temple of the Soul's Retreat built.

Sui Dynasty (581-618)

589 — Qiantang Prefecture is renamed Hangzhou when Emperor Wendi of Sui defeats Chen. The name of Hangzhou is recorded in history books for the first time.

The 1,700-kilometer Grand Canal, the earliest man-made canal dug in the world and the longest, links Beijing with Hangzhou, spurring its economic, agricultural and cultural development.

Tang Dynasty (618-907)

By early Tang Dynasty, Hangzhou has a population of some 100,000.

766 — Hangzhou's development is enhanced by the sink-

ing of six wells diverting drinking water from the West Lake to the city by the court minister, Li Bi, who serves as governor of Hangzhou from 766 to 779.

822 — The poet, Bai Juyi, arrives in Hangzhou to serve as governor and contributes to the place's growth by dredging wells and building causeways in an effort to fight drought and use the lake water to irrigate farmland.

By late Tang, tax on commerce collected in Hangzhou alone constitutes one-twenty-fourth of the total national income.

Phoenix Mosque built.

Five Dynasties and Ten Kingdoms (907-960)

907 — Hangzhou serves as capital of Wuyue after King Qian Liu chooses the region to found his kingdom which lasts 79 years, giving Hangzhou relative stability in a turbulent period. Qian Liu builds a seawall in 910 to contain the Qiantang River, develops sea transportation and establishes ties with Japan, Korea and India.

A city wall of 25 kilometers with 10 gates is built.

970 — Six Harmonies Pagoda constructed.

Amitabha Buddha, Guanyin (the Goddess of Mercy) and Mahasthamaprapta Boddhisattva carved at the Peak That Flew from Afar at Temple of Soul's Retreat which is expanded to include 3,000 monks. Many other temples built to give Hangzhou the name "Kingdom of Buddhism".

Baochu Pagoda built.

Northern Song (960-1127)

1071 — Poet-governor Su Dongpo first arrives in Hangzhou to serve as deputy governor for three years; later returns in 1089 as governor. His contributions include building the Su Causeway, dredging canals and restoring the six wells.

Southern Song (1127-1279)

1130 — General Yue Fei reoccupies Nanjing. In 1142 he is murdered.

1127 — Hangzhou becomes the capital for 153 years and functions as the nation's political, cultural and economic center.

The Southern Song Court builds and expands at Phoenix Hill its palace and city surrounded by a city wall nine meters high, three meters wide and a moat of about 40 meters in width. Over 100 magnificent and majestic halls, pavilions, towers and terraces of various sizes stand on the palace ground of about 25 square kilometers. In addition, 37 temporary palaces and 11 imperial parks dot the area within and around Hangzhou. Several hundred pleasure boats are made for the royal family and court officials. After much renovation and construction, the lake area looks more beautiful than before, giving rise to the "Ten Views of West Lake". The population of Hangzhou passes 1,000,000. Shipbuilding, chinaware, weaving, paper-making, printing and munitions enterprises thrive in Hangzhou. Marco Polo, the Italian traveler, writes that there are 12 different trades in Hangzhou and 12,000 households working in each trade.

The development of handicraft industry helps bring prosperity in commerce. Shops line both sides of the city's streets and lanes. Four-hundred-and-forty different types of markets operate on fixed dates, including markets of medicine, flowers, jewelry, rice, meat, fish, cloth and pigs. The appearance of a kind of check with the same function of copper coins as official money in 1160 testifies to the progress of finance.

The development of commerce, in turn, gives impetus to transportation. Cargo boats call at and leave the various ports on both sides of the Qiantang River at Hangzhou and merchants come and go in their business exchanges.

The number of students rises sharply. At the Imperial Academy, an official institute of higher learning, there are over 4,000 students, more than any time before. At other schools, hundreds of students are engaged in special studies such as military art, mathematics, medicine and calligraphy. There are 17 theaters in the city for the performance of traditional operas and acrobatics. (The paintings of the Imperial Southern Song Academy, woodblock prints of the "Ten Views of West Lake" and Buddhist classics, and porcelain from the Southern Song Official Kiln survive today to testify to the mature culture developed in Hangzhou during the Southern Song.)

1221 — Yue Fei's Temple built.

The Guanyin and Mahasthamaprapta Boddhisattva at Haze at Sunset Cave carved.

Yuan (1279-1368)

The wars ending the Southern Song Dynasty destroy or damage many important Hangzhou buildings. The national political center moves north but Hangzhou remains an important city of southeastern China as the seat of the provincial government.

Hangzhou continues to serve as a major trading port with foreign countries.

Crane Pavilion built in honor of Northern Song poet Lin Hejing (967-1028).

1275-1292 — Marco Polo visits China and sends back to the West glowing reports about Hangzhou, calling it "the finest and most magnificent city in the world".

Ming (1368-1644)

Silk industry and tourism develop. As a center of textile industry and commerce, Hangzhou sees its first few rich silk industry workshop owners with capital amounting to "several scores of thousand taels of gold".

Qing (1644-1911)

1648 — Qing army "Banner Camp" established in Hangzhou.

Emperor Kangxi makes Hangzhou his vacation home and inscribes steles at the "Ten Views of West Lake" and other historic sites.

Hangzhou suffers much damage when imperialist powers invade China in the wake of the Opium War (1840-42) and reduce China to a semi-feudal and semi-colonial country.

1860-64 — The Taipings occupy Hangzhou twice during the Taiping Peasant War (1851-64). (Relics of the site of the Taiping royal government remain in the city at Xiaoying Lane.)

Before the Revolution of 1911, Qiu Jin, Xu Xilin and

other members of revolutionary parties are active in Hangzhou.

The Republic of China (1912-1949)

1921 — Communist Party of China founded. The official Party publication, *Guide*, uses the Hangzhou School of Politics and Law as one of its distribution centers.

1937-45 — Japanese occupation. Many sites looted and damaged.

May 1949 — Hangzhou liberated by the People's Liberation Army.

The People's Republic of China (founded in 1949)

Major restoration work undertaken at West Lake historic sites, reforestation of surrounding hills, extensive building in the city.

1966-76 — "Cultural revolution". During the years of turmoil, parks are closed and suffer damage.

1978 — Hangzhou is named with Beijing, Suzhou and Guilin as one of the four major tourist cities in China.

With a population of 1.1 million, Hangzhou — besides its traditional light, textile and handicraft industries — has an iron and steel industry, machine tool factories, petrochemical and oil refining facilities and an electronics industry. Home of Zhejiang University, Hangzhou University, and other institutions of higher learning, Hangzhou is the capital of Zhejiang Province.

The West Lake *(Xi Hu)*

According to legend, the lake was formed when a pearl, polished in heaven by the Jade Dragon and the Golden Phoenix, fell to earth and turned into the West Lake. The Jade Dragon and Golden Phoenix also fell during a struggle over the gem with the Celestial Empress to become Jade Emperor Hill (*Yuhuang Shan*) and Phoenix Hill (*Fenghuang Shan*), guardians of the lake.[1]

The scientific explanation has been given by the Chinese scientist Zhu Kezhen (1890-1974), who wrote in *The*

---

[1] For a further description of this and other legends see *Folk Tales of the West Lake*, adapted by Wang Hui-Ming, Foreign Languages Press, Beijing, 1982.

Birth and Formation of the West Lake at Hangzhou: "Suppose we could imagine the conditions of the time of the initial formation of the Qiantang River, before the alluvial soil had been deposited. The site of modern Hangzhou would still be an expanse of sea and the West Lake no more than a small bay just near the river mouth. Later, sediment gradually blocked the mouth of the bay to form a lagoon."

West Lake has had different names over the centuries. During the Han Dynasty, when a golden ox was said to have emerged from the lake as a "happy omen for a splendid imperial reign", the lake was called both Golden Ox Lake (*Jinniu Hu*) and Splendid Reign Lake (*Mingsheng Hu*). Since it is on the Qiantang River (*Qiantang Jiang*), it has been called Qiantang Lake (*Qiantang Hu*). After poet-governor Bai Juyi (772-846) built a stone culvert here to release water from the lake, it became known as Stone Culvert Lake (*Shihan Hu*). The poet-governor Su Dongpo (1037-1101) also contributed a name when he compared the lake to a classic beauty, Xi Zi, and the lake took on that poetic name. But generally, the lake is known as West Lake, simply because it lies west of Hangzhou.

The Ten Views of West Lake

The "Ten Views of West Lake" originated some 700 years ago from titles of popular landscape paintings of West Lake scenes produced by the Southern Song Imperial Art Academy. They are: Melting Snow at Broken Bridge, (*Duanqiao Canxue*), Autumn Moon on Calm Lake (*Pinghu Qiuyue*), Three Pools Mirroring the Moon (*Santan Yinyue*), Twin Peaks Piercing the Clouds (*Shuangfeng Cha-*

21

yun), Lotus in the Breeze at Crooked Courtyard (*Quyuan Fenghe*), Spring Dawn by Su Causeway (*Sudi Chunxiao*), Viewing Fish at Flower Harbor (*Huagang Guanyu*), Late Bell at Nanping Hill (*Nanping Wanzhong*), Evening Sunlight at Thunder Peak Pagoda (*Leifeng Xizhao*), and Listening to Orioles Singing in the Willows (*Liulang Wenying*). Forming pairs — for instance, Autumn Moon on Calm Lake goes with Spring Dawn by Su Causeway while Three Pools Mirroring the Moon goes with Twin Peaks Piercing the Clouds — the sites were further established in the Qing Dynasty when Emperor Kangxi visited them and inscribed their names, making errors in the process such as calling Brewery Courtyard "Crooked" Courtyard.

However, the "Ten Views" are recognized not so much for their scenery — many places on the lake are equally impressive — as from the traditional custom in China of having at least 10 views at a site to make it truly formidable. The word "ten" used in this way goes beyond its numerical value to indicate "many". In fact, today the bell no longer sounds at "Late Bell at Nanping Hill", and "Evening Sunlight at Thunder Peak Pagoda" is in ruins. "Lotus in the Breeze at Crooked Courtyard" is a tiny out-of-the-way place which the Parks Administration plans to expand to make it more in keeping with its reputation as a "view". Because of clouds or haze, it is often difficult to see the surrounding hills from the pavilion next to Hongchun Bridge (*Hongchun Qiao*) known as "Twin Peaks Piercing the Clouds".

The custom of giving 10 names in China was satirized by the 20th century writer Lu Xun in an essay he wrote on the collapse of Thunder Peak Pagoda in 1924:

"Many of us in China — here I want to make it quite clear that I do not include all of our four hundred million compatriots — have a sort of 'ten-sight disease' or at least an 'eight-sight disease', which reached epidemic proportions in the Qing Dynasty, I should say. Look through any county annals, and you will find the district has ten sights, if not eight, such as 'Moonlight on a Distant Village,' 'Quiet Monastery and Clear Bell,' 'Ancient Pool and Crystal Water.' ... There are ten sorts of sweetmeats, ten different dishes, ten movements in music, ten courts for the king of hell, ten cures in medicine, ten guesses for the drinking game, even announcements of guilty deeds or crimes usually list ten items, as if no one would stop at nine. Now one of the ten sights of the West Lake is missing."[1]

The seven-storied Thunder Peak (*Lei-feng*) Pagoda built in 975 collapsed on September 25, 1924 after it was weakened over the years by the custom of local people to take a brick from its lower stories as a souvenir or talisman. Inside the structure were found Buddhist scriptures written on silk. One of the bricks and the scroll contained in it can be seen in the Zhejiang

---

[1] Lu Xun, *Selected Works*, translated by Yang Xianyi and Gladys Yang, Volume II, pp. 113-114, Foreign Languages Press, Beijing, 1980.

Museum. The preface to the scriptures reads in translation: "The Great General of the Army, the King of Wuyue, Qian Chu had this 84,000-volume scripture made and placed in the brick pagoda by the west gate to consecrate it forever in this eighth month of the year Yihai."

Lu Xun was not much impressed with the view from Thunder Peak Pagoda when he visited it before its collapse, and he welcomed its demise to the extent that the pagoda symbolized feudalism. However, the way the pagoda was destroyed disturbed him:

"When a Chinese rebel appears, there is a brief commotion. Then he is asked to be the ruler, or a different ruler is found, and the old traditions are patched up amid the ruins. . . .

"Such vandalism simply leaves ruins behind: it has nothing to do with construction.

"But does that mean that there is no destruction in time of peace, when we patch up our old traditions untroubled by invaders and bandits? No, indeed, for then slaves are ceaselessly undermining society.

". . . Take the collapse of Leifeng Pagoda — all we know is that it was owing to the superstition of the country people. The pagoda which was common property was gone, but the country people are left with only a brick apiece, and these bricks will later be hoarded by other selfish people until they all turn to dust. If times are prosperous, and the ten-sight disease is rife, I suppose a new Leifeng Pagoda may be built. But its fate is easy to guess if the country folk remain the same and the old ways remain unchanged.

"Such slavish destruction simply leaves ruins behind: it has nothing to do with construction. . . .

24

"What is distressing is not the ruins, but the fact that the old traditions are being patched up over the ruins. We want wreckers who will bring about reforms, for their hearts are lit up by an ideal. We must learn to distinguish between them and the bandits or slaves, and must beware lest we slip into one of the last categories."[1]

Today in Hangzhou, there is discussion about rebuilding the Leifeng Pagoda. Detractors argue against it, citing Lu Xun's reference to it as a symbol of feudal society. Others feel its scenic value as a counterbalance to Baochu Pagoda across the lake and its historical importance — especially through its association with Hangzhou's most famous love story, *Lady White Snake*, warrant its rebuilding.

Lady White Snake has many versions. Lu Xun himself wrote: "... of all the vaunted beauty spots of the West Lake, the first I heard of was Leifeng Pagoda. My grandmother often told me that Lady White Snake was a prisoner underneath it."[2] As Lu Xun recounts the famous tale as told to him by his grandmother, a man once rescued two snakes, one white and one green. Later, to repay this man's kindness, the white snake changed into a woman and married him while the green snake turned into her maid. But a Buddhist monk by the name of Fahai recognized the woman as a snake, put her under a begging bowl, buried the bowl and built a pagoda over it — Leifeng Pagoda — to prevent her from escaping.

Lu Xun has no patience with the monk's meddling: "A monk should stick to chanting his sutras. If the white snake chose to bewitch (the man) and (he) chose to marry

[1] Lu Xun, *Selected Works, op. cit.*, Volume II, pp. 117-118.
[2] Lu Xun, *Selected Works, op. cit.*, Volume II, p. 100.

a monster, what business was that of anybody else? Yet he had to set down his sutra and stir up trouble. I expect he was jealous — in fact, I am sure of it."[1]

One reason Lu Xun tells us he was glad to hear about the collapse of the pagoda is that his grandmother's version of the story had left Lady White Snake trapped under it. Others believe the woman's maid finally came to rescue her and the meddlesome monk was forced to hide in a crab shell where he lives to this day.

Opposite the remains of the Thunder Peak Pagoda is Pure Benevolence Temple (*Jingci Si*) of Nanping Hill, dating back to 954, which has been built and rebuilt several times since the Southern Song Dynasty. Destroyed during the Taiping Peasant War in the 19th century, one of its largest halls — one-storied, multi-eaved with a yellow glazed tile roof — was repaired in 1955.

Another former site, White Cloud Nunnery (*Baiyun An*) near the ruins of Thunder Peak Pagoda on Nanping Hill served as a revolutionary base in the late Qing Dynasty after the monk in charge, Deshan, joined the revolutionary party in 1902. Xu Xilin, who was later executed for assassinating En Ming, the provincial governor of Anhui, Qiu Jin, the woman revolutionary who was executed in 1907, and others met here in 1906. After 1909, White Cloud Nunnery became the secret general office for the revolution in Zhejiang which brought Dr. Sun Yat-sen there one evening in September 1910. Following the success of the Revolution of 1911, Dr. Sun Yat-sen returned to White Cloud Nunnery in April 1913 to write a plaque to commemorate the role played by the monk Deshan, who after playing his part in the revolution, retired to live as

---

[1] Lu Xun, *Selected Works, op. cit.,* Volume II, p. 101.

a hermit at an old temple in Haining County, Zhejiang Province.

Su Causeway (*Su Di*)

(One of the "Ten Views")

The 2.8-kilometer-long Su Causeway — lined with peach, willow, magnolia, osmanthus and hibiscus along a modern road crossing six single-arch stone bridges — has spanned the West Lake from north to south since it was first constructed in the 11th century by the Northern Song poet-official Su Dongpo for whom it is named.

One of China's most distinguished poets, Su Dongpo, like the Tang poet Bai Juyi, came to make lasting contributions to Hangzhou after having problems at central court which sent him to the provinces. Su Dongpo first served from 1071-73 as deputy governor and later returned in 1089 to serve two years as governor of Hangzhou.

On his first visit, Su Dongpo found West Lake in bad shape. Neglected from the beginning of the Song Dynasty (960), it had become so overgrown with weeds that 20-30 percent of the lake area had been turned into fields. By 1089 when he returned as governor, Su Dongpo found more than half the surface area of the lake dried up. The situation worsened under a severe drought during the first year of his term in office as governor. The following year, he petitioned the court to be allowed to develop the lake in order to provide water for drinking, irrigation, transport and wine-making — all of which had been important services provided by the West Lake. He also asked consideration for the West Lake's scenic beauty: "Hangzhou without West Lake is like a man without eyebrows and eyes. How could a man be without them?"

That summer until autumn some 200,000 workers cleared the undergrowth, using the mud and debris to build what is now known as the Su Causeway, spanning the surface of the lake from the north to the south. Small stone pagodas were erected to mark areas of the lake where it was forbidden to grow water plants to avoid future clogging of the lake. These pagodas were forerunners of today's "Three Pagodas Reflecting the Moon", or more commonly referred to as the "Three Pools Mirroring the Moon". By the time Su Dongpo left Hangzhou, the lake had been restored, and he could write some of his best known lines:

"Shimmering water at its full, sunny day best.
Blurred mountains in a haze — marvelous even in rain.
Compare West Lake to the beautiful woman Xi Zi:
She looks just as becoming
Lightly made up or richly adorned."

Broken Bridge (*Duan Qiao*)

(One of the "Ten Views")

This single-arch vaulted bridge has had various names over the years but the present one — which first appeared

(Previous page)

Top: The thawing snow at Broken Bridge

Middle: West Lake after a rain

Bottom: One of the three pagodas in the mid-lake first built in the 17th century

A bird's-eye view of West Lake

Mist-shrouded lake water
and   weeping   willows

Spring   comes   to   Three
Pools   Mirroring the Moon

in a Tang Dynasty poem — comes from the Bai Causeway's being "broken" or ended at the bridge on the city side. Serving as a demarcation line for Inner West Lake (*Li Xi Hu*) and Outer West Lake (*Wai Xi Hu*), the bridge also plays an important role in the best known folktale associated with Hangzhou, *Lady White Snake*, about a white snake which changes itself into a beautiful woman who falls in love with a young man. The snake-woman and the young man meet each other for the first time near Broken Bridge.

Three Pools Mirroring the Moon

(*Santan Yinyue*)

(One of the "Ten Views")

Boats can be taken from the north bank of the West Lake — either individual rowboats or a motorboat, powered by batteries to avoid pollution, which seats 12 people — onto the lake where the chief attraction is Lesser Yingzhou Isle (*Xiao Yingzhou*) with a view known as Three Pools Mirroring the Moon. On the way, two smaller isles, also man-made, are passed: Mid-Lake Pavilion (*Huxin Ting*) built in the Ming Dynasty and reconstructed in 1952 which has a teahouse and a good view of the lake, and Ruan Yuan's Mound (*Ruangong Dun*), the smallest of the lake's islands which was built from lake-bottom silt in 1800 under the supervision of Zhejiang Viceroy Ruan Yuan and which stood for many years as a wildlife refuge since the soil was too mucky to support buildings. In April 1982, the Hangzhou Parks Administration topped the isle with over 1,000 tons of earth to provide a foundation for some 240-square meters of bamboo halls and pavilions and a paved road which now encircles the island. Over 600 flowers and shrubs were also planted as part of the project to create a new scenic site — dominated by a fishing terrace — on the lake.

Lesser Yingzhou Isle was built in 1607 with dredgings from the lake which created a lake within a lake and an island within an island. The site covers approximately 17 acres (nearly seven hectares), of which about 60 percent is water surface, with four inner pools surrounded by landscape with scores of plants and flowers including several varieties of rose, lilac, white magnolia, crab apple and willow. A zigzag concrete bridge, Nine-Bend Bridge (*Jiuqu Qiao*), connects the inner isle with the shore, leading past an unusual three-pillared pavilion, a Taihu Lake style rock, Nine-Lion Rock (*Jiushi Shi*), and a  three-cornered pavilion. On one side, a white-washed wall with a moon-gate stands before a bamboo grove — a traditional spot for picture taking. The concrete walk-way leads past a stele which is inscribed with the characters announcing "Three Pools Mirroring the Moon" written by the Qing Emperor Kangxi. Broken during the "cultural revolution", it has been repaired with a seam along its center.

The pavilion on the south side of Lesser Yingzhou Isle has calligraphy from the Chan (Zen) Buddhist Sect which in translation reads "Heart-Linking-to-Heart", reflecting the Zen meaning: "Since all can be sensed, there is no need to speak." The three 17th-century stone pagodas rising from the lake in front of the pavilion got their name from the moon casting its reflection through the holes in the pagodas as three moons on the water. They are said to have originally been placed in the lake to indicate a zone in which it was forbidden to plant lotus to prevent the lake from becoming overgrown. Today the lotus plants fill the inner lakes of the isle with their scarlet, pink and white blossoms.

Lotus today are cultivated in Hangzhou not only for their beauty but also as a food — nearly all parts of the lotus can be eaten raw or cooked, while the lotus root is processed into a starch from which is made the porridge served at all the teahouses in the area. The lotus is also said to have medicinal value with the seeds having sedative properties, the tassel restoring energy, the core acting as a diuretic, and the petals promoting blood circulation. Harvest seasons are from late July until August and from early September until late October.

Solitary Hill Island (*Gu Shan*)

An off-shoot of Qixia Ridge (*Qixia Ling*), 35-meter-high Solitary Hill (*Gu Shan*) is surrounded by water on all sides, standing alone in the northern part of West Lake. Its many plum trees also have given it the name of Plum Blossom Islet (*Meihua Yu*).

Solitary Hill Island

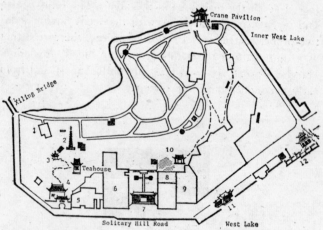

1 Wu Changshuo Memorial Hall
2 Pagoda of Avatamsaka Sutra
3 Stone House for the Funerary Stele of "Sanlao"
4 Xiling Seal-Engraving Society
5 Louwailou Restaurant
6 Zhejiang Provincial Library

7 Sun Yat-sen Park
8 Hall of Flourishing Literature
9 Zhejiang Provincial Museum
10 "The Most Beautiful Spot of West Lake"
11 Blue Lake and Sky
12 Autumn Moon on Calm Lake

Xiling Bridge (*Xiling Qiao*)

The single-arch Xiling Bridge stretches across the foot of Qixia Ridge to Solitary Hill. Opposite the site of the white marble statue of the revolutionary woman hero Qiu Jin (1877-1907) on the other side of the bridge there used to stand the tomb of Su Xiaoxiao (479-501), a courtesan native of Hangzhou known for her beauty and talent. While sight-seeing in her carriage along the lakeside one day, she is said to have met and fallen in love at first sight with a young man, Ruan Yu. She composed this poem on the spot:

"I in a covered carriage,
You on a gray steed.
Where did our hearts meet?
Beneath the pines at Xiling."

Her tomb was removed in 1964 along with several other tombs of both real and legendary people that used to stand along West Lake. Several of these tombs of anti-feudal revolutionaries — including Xu Xilin, Ma Zonghan, Chen Boping, Shen Youzhi, Yang Zheshang, and Tao Chengzhang — have been rebuilt at a site near West Lake on the road to Dragon Well. A pavilion in memory of Su Xiaoxiao is being built at the former site of her tomb.

Xiling Seal-Engraving Society (*Xiling Yinshe*)

A lovely view of the lake from the top of Solitary Hill after a climb through a classical Chinese garden with springs and pavilions is among the attractions of the Xiling Seal-Engraving Society, founded in 1913 to "preserve seal-cutting and conduct research into the art". The society itself has over 100 members, skilled calligraphers who are engaged in the practice and study of the ancient art of inscribing characters in stone or metal. The art reached its peak in the 1700s when a native of Hangzhou, Ding Jing, founded a school merging the arts of calligraphy and engraving. Several pavilions along the climb up the hill contain examples of the work of famous seal-engravers.  A collection of seals given to the society by Li Shutong, an engraver who decided in 1918 to become a monk, is entombed behind a plaque in the hill's rockface.

Many foreign visitors like to buy their own seal or "chop" engraved with an appropriate Chinese name which can be supplied by an interpreter at the society. There are a number of pattern books from which to choose the style as well as the kind of stone, including bloodstone, jade, agate or crystal. Prices for stones vary from a few cents to several thousand yuan. According to Li Xinbing, a salesperson at the shop, following the "cultural revolution", a new wave of interest among young Chinese in the old cultural traditions has created a great demand for chops and books on seal-engraving.

Among the most famous of the buildings at the Xiling Seal-Engraving Society is the Bamboo Chamber (*Zhu Ge*) built by Bai Juyi during the Tang Dynasty. At the top of the hill is the 11-storied Pagoda of Avatamsaka Sutra (*Hua-yanjing Ta*), which the monk Hongsan of Virtue Gathering Temple (*Zhaoxian Si*) built in 1924, and a statue of the scholar Ding Jing. Tables are set around where people can enjoy the view while having tea and sweets sold at a shop on the top.

Among the society's prize possessions, kept in a stone house on the hill, is the funerary stele of "*Sanlao*", the title for an official in charge of cultural affairs dating from the early Eastern Han period more than 1,900 years ago. The oldest stele in Hangzhou, it was unearthed at Kexing Hill (*Kexing Shan*) in Yuyao County in 1852 during the Qing Dynasty. The cutting of stone tablets to record events began in the early years of the Eastern Han Dynasty, but inscriptions on tombs noting the name of the deceased and dates of birth and death generally did not appear on graves until the end of that period. Since this stele does record the time of death of an official, "*Sanlao*", in a style of calligraphy which is both Qin and Han, it provides an important reference for studying the origin and development of stone engraving and tomb inscriptions.

Sun Yat-sen Park (*Zhongshan Gongyuan*)

The Sun Yat-sen Park, named after the leader of the Revolution of 1911, combines woods, pavilions and terraces, small bridges over running water and winding paths along the side of Solitary Hill. The park, along with Zhejiang Provincial Museum next door, is laid out on the former grounds of emperors' palaces and gardens, first built in 1252, during the Song Dynasty. A vacation palace was also built during the Qing Dynasty when Emperor Kangxi frequently visited West Lake. Later on the area was turned into a temple, and in 1927, was renamed Sun Yat-sen Park. Two places in the park are considered particularly impressive — an area of crooked bridges, pools, and plants and pavilions designated as "The Most Beautiful Spot of West Lake" and an area of ornamental rocks at the top of Solitary Hill called "The Green Cloud Path".

Zhejiang Provincial Museum
(Zhejiang Bowuguan)

Built in 1929, the Zhejiang Provincial Museum exhibits historical finds in Zhejiang Province. Also located on the former site of the vacation palace of the Qing emperors, the grounds include a stream flowing through a classical Chinese garden of trees and rocks.

Among the artifacts displayed at the museum are 7,000-year-old bone farm tools discovered in 1973 at Hemudu site, Yuyao County, Zhejiang Province, a vast flat river valley of 40,000 square meters. The many ancient paddy-fields discovered at the site proved that the people of Hemudu used plowing tools for rice cultivation. This is 2,000 years earlier than the common assumption of the time when plowing tools were first used. The discovery of the remains of many wooden-framed buildings along with the unearthing of spinning implements and pottery with carved designs shows that the ancient Chinese had created a flourishing primitive culture which was not confined to the basin of the Huanghe (Yellow) River but went beyond to the Changjiang (Yangtze) and perhaps even farther.

Among the relics at the museum from the Neolithic period 4,000 to 5,000 years ago are Liangzhu black pottery and jadework from Liangzhu, 18 kilometers northwest of Hangzhou. Valuable items among the Shang and Zhou dynasties' bronzeware on exhibit include a Shang bronze vessel found at Anji County, a Shang bronze steamer from Haiyan County, and large bronze cymbals from the Western Zhou period unearthed at Changxing County. The museum has a large collection of bronze swords from the Spring and Autumn Period (770-476 B.C.) and the Warring States Period (475-221 B.C.). Many of the bronzes are still bright, indicating the advanced corrosion-proofing treatment of the time.

Mirrors make up the greater part of the museum's collection of copperware. Of these, the mirrors produced at Shaoxing during the Eastern Han decorated with chariots and horses are the best known. Among the most popular of the time were mirrors depicting the legendary Queen Mother of the West as she sat with the King Father of the East attended by servants while galloping horses pulled them in a chariot with fine silk streaming behind.

Visitors can try their hand at rubbing the handles of the "Basin of Spouting Fish" to hear a ringing sound and watch water jump up in small fountains from the vibration. The basin is believed to be a product before the Ming Dynasty.

The Zhejiang Provincial Museum also has a large collection of ancient celadonware made in the province, porcelain from the Longquan Kiln which was one of the five great kilns in China during the Song Dynasty, collections of old paintings, drawings, calligraphy of famous people, inscriptions on ancient bronzes and stones, handicraft articles, wood blocks for printing and coins.

Also on the grounds of the Zhejiang Provincial Museum is the Hall of Flourishing Literature (*Wenlan Ge*), built in 1782 in the Qing Dynasty as one of seven large libraries to house the *Complete Library of the Four Treasures of Knowledge* (*Siku Quanshu*), the most comprehensive collection of books of 3,000 years — since the time China had writing — on philosophy, politics, science and technology, medicine, literature, mathematics and astronomy. The project was begun in 1773 during the reign of Qing Emperor Qianlong and was completed in 1782. In 1861, part of the collection was lost in a fire but restoration began in 1880 to collect and copy the lost and incomplete volumes. This went on even after the Revolution of 1911 until the collection was finally restored. During the Qing

compilation work, the old forms were tampered with and essays from the past were altered which caused Lu Xun to remark in his *Essays from Qiejieting*: The collection "was compiled by the Qing and the classics disappeared". Nevertheless, the book collection — now stored in the nearby Zhejiang Library on Solitary Hill — remains a valuable part of classical Chinese literature. The whole work includes more than 36,000 volumes classified according to content, covered in different colored silks, and stored in 6,752 boxes. This includes 79,070 books written throughout in neat Chinese script on 2,300,000 pages.

Originally, four sets of the collection were made and stored in literary halls built specially to house them in Beijing, Chengde and Shenyang. Later three other sets were made to be stored in halls at Yangzhou, Zhenjiang and Hangzhou. Today the set in Hangzhou is the only one left south of Changjiang and of the literary halls, only the ones at Beijing, Shenyang, Chengde and Hangzhou remain, the largest one being in Hangzhou. In excellent condition, the Hall of Flourishing Literature is now used to house the museum's special exhibitions.

Crane Pavilion (*Fanghe Ting*)

From Xiling Bridge, a short walk along Inner West Lake (*Li Xi Hu*) past plum trees — which create a "fragrant snow" when they bloom in winter — leads to the Crane Pavilion on the north slope of Solitary Hill. The pavilion, rebuilt in 1915, is in memory of the Northern Song poet, Lin Hejing (967-1028), who lived as a recluse on the hill with a crane as a companion. It may have been near this spot that Lin Hejing wrote an especially admired poem, two lines of which read in translation:

"Sparse plum branches cast
Their clear reflection on the shallow water.
Subtle fragrance comes and goes
Under a pale moon."

One calligraphy at the pavilion praises Lin Hejing for refusing to write anything for the royal court; another reads in translation: "Because of the plums, Solitary Hill is no longer solitary." It is said the poet planted 365 plum trees on the hill, each day selling the seeds from one tree to make a living. Inside the pavilion is a carving of "Poem to the Dancing Crane", a work of the Southern and Northern Dynasties in the calligraphy of the Qing Emperor Kangxi in the style of the famous calligrapher Dong Qichang.

Autumn Moon on Calm Lake
(*Pinghu Qiuyue*)
(One of the "Ten Views")

This teahouse with its cement terrace bounded on three sides by water became one of the traditional places to view the West Lake, especially on an autumn night when the moon is full, after a pavilion was built on the location during the Tang Dynasty. In 1699 during the reign of Emperor Kangxi, a repository for royal books was built here with a terrace in front of it. The present structure was rebuilt in 1959.

Bai Causeway (*Bai Di*)

From the city side, Solitary Hill is reached by the Bai Causeway, a one-kilometer-long embankment lined on both sides by plum trees and weeping willows planted at regular intervals. Even over 1,000 years ago in the Tang Dynasty, the Bai Causeway — then known as the Baisha Causeway — was famous for its beautiful scenery. The Tang poet-official Bai Juyi wrote:

"Wild flowers are beginning to dazzle the eye.
The short grass just covers the horses' hooves.
I like most to go east of the lake and linger there
At the Baisha Causeway shaded by green willows."

Although Bai Juyi (772-846) happened not to be responsible for the construction of the causeway, people came to associate his name with it out of respect for him as a poet and for the work he did around the West Lake during the three years (822-24) he served as governor of Hangzhou. In fact, Bai Juyi did supervise the construction of another causeway on the lake which has disappeared.

One of China's most distinguished poets, Bai Juyi, wrote many West Lake poems during his stay in Hangzhou and after his return to the Tang court which helped bring a special distinction to the West Lake area. One of his most famous poems reads in translation:

"Spring comes to the lake — a picture.
The scattered hills surround the water's edge
While pines cover the mountains, green on green.
In the moonlight, the waves enshrine a pearl

And the early rice grows like ends
Of threads on an emerald carpet.
The new rushes fan out like green silk.
One cannot bear to leave Hangzhou —
Part of the reason — this lake."

Sent to Hangzhou as a demotion for having offended the Tang court by his frank poems satirizing court life, Bai Juyi was an effective administrator who is remembered for his concern for the people as expressed in one poem, "On Leaving the People of the Region":

"Taxes are heavy and the poor households many.
The peasants starve and cannot water the parched fields.
There is only the lake to save this ill-starred year."

As governor, Bai Juyi worked to improve the situation in Hangzhou by organizing irrigation projects to store lake water. He had ancient wells dredged, reinforced causeways, diverted water from the lake to irrigate fields and raise the water level so that water could flow more freely among the lake, river and fields. Bai Juyi's detailed notes on these construction projects can be found in his *Notes on Lake and Rock at the Qiantang*.

While supervising these engineering projects which were to have a lasting impact on the area, Bai Juyi found the time to study and develop his art and enjoy leisurely moments composing poems with friends like the monk-poet Taoguang. His own assessment (in the poem, "Leaving a Poem in the Study") of his activities in Hangzhou:

"There is nothing I can do to change habits,
Except perhaps teach the local people to understand poetry."

43

North of the Lake

Yue Fei's Tomb and
Temple (*Yuefen*, *Yuemiao*)

"On March 14, 1961, the State Council of the People's Republic of China declared Yue Fei's Tomb and Temple a major historic relic under the protection of the state."

The translation of the above plaque in Chinese calligraphy to the right of the entrance along the imposing red walls surrounding Yue Fei's Tomb and Temple at the foot of Qixia Ridge (*Qixia Ling*) indicates the significance this impressive site has for Chinese visitors to West Lake.

"All visitors come to respect Yue Fei," said He Qi, on a visit to the temple. "Hangzhou is not just a place of scenic beauty but one of history, and the image of Yue Fei holds an important place in the whole area because he's closely linked with heroes and without these historical figures the lake loses much of its significance. Don't take West Lake as purely a scenic spot — it has a lot to do with history."

General Yue Fei (1103-42), was a Song commander who led an army north against the Jin invaders when Hangzhou was the capital of the Southern Song Dynasty. Despite his success, he was ordered to withdraw by Emperor Gaozong on the advice of his Prime Minister, Qin

Hui, who favored capitulation. Yue Fei was framed, arrested and killed along with his son, on the charge of some "probable" crimes.

Only 21 years later, Yue Fei was exonerated under the force of public opinion and buried with due ceremony. In 1221 a temple was also built to honor Yue Fei at Qixia Ridge. For generations, people have visited here to pay their respects to the hero who was determined to recover the lost territories.

However, the plaque to the left of the entrance tells another story about both the survival of Yue Fei's reputation and the temple itself: "A major relic spot under the protection of the state. Destroyed 1966. Renovated 1979 in one year with 56,000 work days at a cost of 400,000 yuan."

Of all the sites in Hangzhou attacked during the "cultural revolution", Yue Fei's Tomb and Temple suffered the worst destruction. The clay statue of the general was smashed, steles written in his calligraphy were broken and stolen, the kneeling iron-cast figures of the officials who framed Yue Fei disappeared. The only major relics to escape were the ceremonial stone figures which still stand at the tomb, saved by staff of the Hangzhou Parks Administration who buried them before the attack. After the downfall of the "gang of four", local authorities moved quickly to restore the site and today feel that in some ways the present temple — which throughout history has been destroyed and repaired several times with the last major renovation taking place in 1923 — surpasses the old.

Going through the entrance gate, the visitor walks up a path of flag-stones with huge camphor trees on either side to approach the multi-eaved gate of the temple itself above which the plaque decorated with the ancient symbols of power, the dragon and the phoenix, announces in gold print on a black background: "Yue Fei's Temple." His tomb is to the left through a gate on adjacent grounds.

At the center of the main hall, with two rows of 12 red-lacquered pillars at either side, is the 4.54-meter-high statue of Yue Fei, built in plaster by the staff of the Sculpture Department of Zhejiang Fine Arts Institute and based on the traditional style of Chinese colored clay sculpture. The Hangzhou Parks Administration and Cultural Relics Administration which commissioned the work decided to replace the previous Buddha-like statue with a more realistic representation and researched Song Dynasty records to make the portrayal of the general as authentic as possible. He wears a red-tasseled commander's helmet, official purple garb with gold armor and military boots.

Above the statue hangs a plaque in Yue Fei's calligraphy which in translation reads: "Recover Our Lost Territories." Another calligraphy to the sides of the statue is by Zhao Puchu, Chairman of the National Buddhist Association: "The rebuilding of this temple reflects the wishes of the people. With the rebuilding even the cypress in the courtyard is filled with new vitality."

The last line refers to a display of ancient petrified wood in the courtyard symbolizing Yue Fei's loyalty. The myth is that when he was imprisoned the cypress tree outside the jail died but did not rot. Another symbol of purity and loyalty are the some 370 paintings of cranes on the temple's ceiling. Along the walls towards the back of the temple are eight murals representing different aspects of Yue Fei's career which were completed by the staff from the Chinese Painting Department of Zhejiang Fine Arts Institute in 1982.

"They were not part of the original temple design and may look a bit out of place," said Associate Professor Song Zhongyuan, who directed the project. "However, we made sure that the murals would give visitors a true reflection of Yue Fei's life and have presented them in a form Chinese visitors will find easy to appreciate."

The first panel to the right of the statue shows Yue Fei practicing military arts as a youth. The second represents Yue Fei's reoccupation of Nanjing in 1130 which had been given up by the corrupt Song court. The third is titled "Recover Our Lost Territories", representing his determination as he pushed west along the Changjiang and Hanshui rivers to take six prefectural seats, linking up the southeast and northwest of the Southern Song empire. The fourth shows his major victory at Yancheng, Henan Province, in 1140, as citizens there welcomed him after the battle. The young man in gray to his left in this panel is probably his son, Yue Yun.

The fifth panel shows the sadness of the people as Yue Fei, on the orders of the emperor, was forced to retreat. He is reported to have said, "the successes of 10 years are ruined in a day." The sixth panel represents Yue Fei's eight-character response when asked to write a confession: "The sky and sun can see an innocent man." The seventh panel shows Yue Fei as he joined forces with the Liang and Zhao to form a united front against the invaders, bringing various forces together in a common struggle. The last panel, to the left facing Yue Fei's statue, shows his mother as she tattooed four words on her young son's back: "Be loyal to the country."

Behind the main temple is a smaller one which was at one time dedicated to Yue Fei's daughter and is now a teahouse.

The layout of the grounds of the temple is typical of a Song Dynasty garden. Connecting the tomb grounds with the grounds of the main temple are two corridors containing carvings or steles. The northern wing contains Yue Fei's own poems and formal writings while the southern wing contains steles with poems by others throughout history describing their feelings about Yue Fei. Traces of the recent destruction to these steles can be seen, but stone masons, landscape gardeners, artisans and historians have done excellent restoration work throughout the temple.

Forty-five of the original 87 stone tablets in the corridors have been recovered and repaired. Some of Yue Fei's works have been recarved; rubbings of other pieces were especially made and brought here from the Yue Fei Memorial Hall at his hometown in Tangyin County, Henan Province; and 37 pieces have been recarved and 24 steles brought here from the old Yue Fei Temple at Zhong'an Bridge in Hangzhou. Yue Fei's character is revealed in these translated quotes from some of his writings:

— On duty: "How can I concern myself about my family when the enemy remains undefeated?"

— On corruption: "If the state officials were not greedy for money and their military counterparts did not flinch at death, the whole country would be at peace."

— On army discipline: "We'd rather freeze to death than intrude into the people's houses; we'd rather starve to death than plunder."

— On inter-army relationships: "Everybody is for the country, no distinctions should be made."

The entrance to the tomb, reached by crossing a stone bridge, was rebuilt with its arched wing corners according to Southern Song architectural style. On both sides of the funerary path leading to the tomb stand the preserved ceremonial stone guardians — six human figures, two

horses, two tigers and two goats — the full complement allowed someone of Yue Fei's rank. The tigers and goats probably date from the Southern Song Dynasty while the others were added during renovations at the beginning of the Ming Dynasty.

The tombstone, which had previously been a bare dome, was restored in 1979 according to Southern Song style with grass growing on top. To its left is the tomb of Yue Fei's eldest son, Yue Yun.

At the entrance to the grounds facing the tomb are statues of those who conspired to frame and murder Yue Fei and his son: Qin Hui and his wife Wang Shi on one side of the gate; and Mo Qixie, a follower of Qin Hui, and Zhang Jun, a general, on the other. According to records, iron figures of Qin Hui, Wang Shi, and Mo Qixie were first cast in 1513 under the Ming Dynasty but were soon smashed by visitors. In 1594 Fan Lai, a deputy court inspector, had them recast and added a statue of Zhang Jun. Later, Wang Ruxun, the provincial governor who was related to Wang Shi, ordered her statue and that of Zhang Jun sunk in the West Lake. In 1602, Fan Lai, appointed commissioner of Zhejiang, came to Hangzhou again. He then restored the four statues a second time. Repeatedly abused by visitors, the statues were recast several times. After the destruction of Yue Fei's tomb in the autumn of 1966, the four kneeling figures disappeared without a trace. Recast in 1979 when the temple was restored, the figures are based on the iron statues at the Yue Fei Memorial Hall at his home county, Henan Province. Chinese visitors still customarily spit on these statues although a sign admonishes them not to do so.

Another expression of contempt for the four and respect for General Yue Fei is in the calligraphy on the wall behind them next to the entrance which in translation reads:

"The green hills are fortunate to be the burial ground of a loyal general;
The white iron was unfortunate to be cast into the statues of traitors."

Yellow Dragon Cave and Purple Cloud Cave (*Huanglong Dong, Ziyun Dong*)

About an hour's walk takes visitors from the back of Yue Fei's Temple up along a path on Qixia Ridge past several caves down through a bamboo and pine forest to the Yellow Dragon Cave (*Huanglong Dong*). The first cave to be reached after about a 20-minute climb is the Purple Cloud Cave (*Ziyun Dong*), surrounded by peach trees, at a location which offers a good view of the lake and relief from the heat in summer. The oldest natural cave on the ridge, the Purple Cloud Cave — divided into two sections — houses the Seven Treasure Spring (*Qibao Quan*) about one meter square, and three ancient carvings of Buddhas on its rock face whose origins have been lost through time. The words "Purple Cloud Cave Scene" carved on the wall refer to the dark purple color of the rocks in the caves. A place near the cave once had the tomb of Niu Gao, a respected general under Yue Fei's command. Another 15-minute walk leads to the Golden Drum Cave (*Jingu Dong*) which has a large entrance but is not deep. From this point, it is about another 15 minutes down the ridge to the entrance of the Yellow

Dragon Cave which is surrounded by Taoist temple buildings dating from the 13th century, and also recently restored. One set of calligraphy at the entrance gate explains this temple was first a Buddhist temple which later became Taoist. The other set with gold print on blue background eulogizes the Taoist sage, Lao Zi.

It is said that during the Song Dynasty, the Buddhist monk Huikai built a temple here, and one day, following a clap of thunder and an earth tremor, a rock on the mountain split into the shape of a dragon's mouth from which a spring gurgled forth. People concluded that a yellow dragon must have followed Huikai to the spot.

Today a yellow dragon's head is carved into the hill with water streaming from its mouth to land into a pool beneath. Behind it are artificial hills made from unworked yellow sandstone. A path leads up the hill through bamboo to another cave, Sleeping Cloud Cave (*Woyun Dong*). Beneath the dragon is an inscription which reads in translation: "Where there's a dragon, all things are possible."

The bamboo garden on the right side of the temple grows a rare "square" variety of bamboo with rectangular stalks and blunt thorns at its joints.

King Qian Chu Pagoda (*Baochu Ta*)

The King Qian Chu Pagoda, commonly referred to as Baochu Pagoda, is best known for the graceful skyline it creates with Precious Stone Hill (*Baoshi Shan*) on which it stands north of West Lake. This northern skyline once was balanced on the south by the skyline created by Thunder Peak Pagoda on Nanping Hill across the lake until Thunder Peak Pagoda fell down in 1924. Baochu Pagoda was compared to a beauty because of its slim lines while the unsteady Thunder Peak Pagoda was compared to an old monk.

Baochu Pagoda itself has been destroyed and rebuilt many times since it was first constructed, according to historical records, by a minister of the Wuyue Kingdom in the early 10th century. According to legend, it was first built as a symbol to protect Qian Chu, the last ruler of the Wuyue Kingdom, on a trip north. The present 45.3-meter-high brick structure — which cannot be climbed since it has no inner stairwell — was built in 1933.

For those who like to hike, a visit to Baochu Pagoda followed by a walk along a mountain path to Early Sun Terrace, also known as Sunrise Terrace (*Chuyang Tai*), makes a good trek although visitors should be warned that the climb up the stone steps to the top of 78-meter-high Precious Stone Hill is a steep one. Those who take on the challenge can pause to rest at the teahouse near

Baochu Pagoda which has a beautiful view of the city of Hangzhou and the lake. Going west from the pagoda past the Alighting Phoenix Pavilion (*Laifeng Ting*), a path leads towards Geling Hill (*Ge Ling*) through huge boulders of igneous rock, including jasper or "precious rock" of a dark purple color.

Stretching several miles from Precious Stone Hill to Qixia Ridge behind Yue Fei's Tomb, Geling Hill at its highest point — Sunrise Terrace — is more than 125 meters high and an ideal place to see the Qiantang River far to the east stretching to the East China Sea and to watch the sunrise catch the water of West Lake and tinge its morning mist with pink. The hill was named after a Jin Dynasty alchemist, Ge Hong, who is said to have lived and worked here experimenting with making a pill of immortality until he died at the age of 81. The remains of the terrace where he is said to have practiced alchemy can still be seen today.

During the Southern Song Dynasty, Geling Hill was also the home of Jia Sidao, the prime minister to the Song court with its capital in Hangzhou, who is held as one of those responsible for the fall of the Southern Song Dynasty in 1279. While the besieged army and people under the Song fought against the intrusion of Yuan soldiers, Jia Sidao is said to have ignored reports from the front to engage in cricket fights in the company of concubines at his pleasure palaces on Geling Hill. Jia Sidao was finally assassinated on his way to exile. His memory survives in the traditional opera, "Story of Red Plum", in which the villain of the piece, Jia Sidao, is based on the historical figure.

West of the Lake

Viewing Fish at Flower Harbor
(*Huagang Guanyu*)
(One of the "Ten Views")

Visitors often follow up Three Pools Mirroring the Moon with a trip to Viewing Fish at Flower Harbor at Flower Harbor Park, commonly referred to as Huagang Park near the south end of the Su Causeway. Originally built as the private garden of a Song Dynasty court attendant, it remained a famous garden spot through the Qing Dynasty but had fallen into disrepair through years of neglect before the Liberation of 1949. Since that time, extensive improvements have been made to develop a 55-acre (about 22 hectares) park with many varieties of trees and flowers, featuring a peony garden which blooms in April and a goldfish pond which is the famous site for viewing fish. Well-stocked with gold carp, the pond attracts many visitors who linger to watch and feed the fish with the bait they bring or buy from the stand beside the pond.

A winding path through a beautifully worked mound of ornamental hills with sculpted pines surrounding the Peony Pavilion (*Mudan Ting*), leads to the Peony Garden,

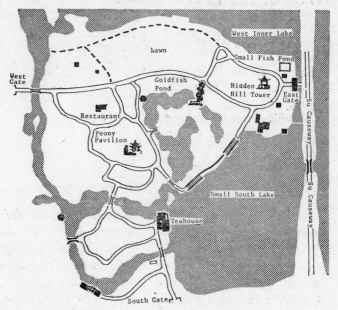

the park's centerpiece where in April many colors of rare peonies bloom in plots separated by black and white cobblestones laid out in the pattern of plum blossoms.

The growing of peonies in Hangzhou dates back centuries. Su Dongpo often mentioned them in his poems and once referred to the 1,000 peony plants of several hundred varieties growing in the garden, indicating the scale of peony cultivation in Hangzhou in his time.

The clear waters of Flower Harbor, built since the Liberation, connect West Inner Lake (*Xi Li Hu*) and Small South Lake (*Xiao Nan Hu*) and enclose the whole "Viewing Fish at Flower Harbor" garden. Following the ins and outs of Flower Harbor, in the southern part of the park, is an azalea ornamental rock garden.

Temple of the Soul's Retreat (*Lingyin Si*)

One of the largest Buddhist temples in southeast China and a national cultural treasure, the 1,600-year-old Temple of the Soul's Retreat, also known as Lingyin Temple or Monastery of the Spirits' Retreat, is nestled in the woods across from a hill with important examples — over 300 rock carvings dating from between the 10th and 14th centuries — of sculptural art in south China.

The original temple is said to have been built in A.D. 326 by an Indian monk, Huili, whose remains are contained in the nine-meter-high, hexagonal seven-storied Monk Huili Pagoda (*Ligong Ta*), rebuilt in 1590, near the entrance to the temple grounds. Next to the pagoda sits Monk Huili Rock (*Ligong Yan*) with a Sanskrit inscription: "There is a piece of jade within the lotus flower."

A path from the entrance along the stream separating the temple from the carvings on the cliff-face of the Peak That Flew from Afar (*Feilai Feng*) leads several hundred yards to the temple complex itself where there stand two pillars with Buddhist inscriptions in front of the temple erected in 969 A.D. by the King of Wuyue, Qian Chu.

Ruined and rebuilt many times over the centuries, Lingyin Temple went under large-scale construction in the 10th century when the ruler of the Five Dynasties' Wuyue Kingdom was converted to Buddhism. At that time the temple consisted of 9 buildings, 18 pavilions, over 72 halls and 1,300 rooms for 3,000 monks. The present temple structures, including its two main halls — the Hall of the Four Heavenly Kings (*Tianwang Dian*) in the front and behind it the main Grand Hall (*Daxiong Baodian*) — were extensively restored in the early 1950s. During the "cultural revolution", some rock carvings suffered minor damage but the temple was spared major destruction after Premier Zhou Enlai ordered the place closed and protected. The temple was closed from 1968 to 1979.

Today some 63 monks and 70 other staff members manage the temple, the only active Buddhist temple in Hangzhou under the auspices of the Buddhist Society.

"Before the 'cultural revolution', the Buddhist Society of Hangzhou had 28 temples under its management but because of the sabotage of the 'gang of four' most of them were occupied by other units," said Yu Yongxi, Secretary-General of Hangzhou Buddhist Society, in an office off a side garden at the temple which also features a vegetarian restaurant. Among the prominent foreign Buddhists who have come to Lingyin Temple, Prince Norodom Sihanouk, President of Democratic Kampuchea, has visited several times.

"The emperor made a mistake here," said Sun Jiasui, an editor familiar with ancient poetry as he looked up at the plaque above the main temple entrance inscribed by the Qing Emperor Kangxi. Apparently, the emperor enjoyed visiting West Lake sites and composing poems about them but often made mistakes, including the inscription at one of the "Ten Views" where a stele stands in his calligraphy announcing the "Crooked" courtyard instead of the "Brewery" courtyard. An inscription on the back by his grandson attempts to explain the mistakes his grandfather made.

At Lingyin, the story goes that when he was asked to honor the temple with his calligraphy, Emperor Kangxi wrote the top part of the first character *yu* — which is only one-third of the character for "soul" — so large that it covered half the space. To cover his error, he simply filled the remaining space by adding the character with *yun*, creating the graph which means "cloud". So instead of being properly announced as Temple of the Soul's Retreat, the calligraphy above the temple reads "Monastery for Meditation in the Cloud Forest" (*Yunlin Chansi*).

In the front Hall of the Four Heavenly Kings, barechested Maitreya Buddha sits in the center of the building. Behind, in a niche stands the temple guardian with a stern expression holding a pestle for destroying demons. Carved from a whole piece of camphor wood, the figure is more than 700 years old, dating back to the Southern Song Dynasty. Along the walls at either side are four large seated figures of the Heavenly Kings, said to symbolize good weather and peace.

A path flanked by age-old trees in the middle of a spacious courtyard leads to the second hall in the temple, the Grand Hall which, 33.6 meters in height, is a multi-eaved, single-storied structure in three layers. The hall was renovated in 1954 when it was reinforced with cement and its roof reinforced with iron and steel to prevent further destruction by white ants. The statue of Sakyamuni, 19.6 meters high and carved from 24 blocks of camphor wood, was constructed in 1956 by folk artists and sculptors from Zhejiang Fine Arts Institute. Based on a carving from the Tang Dynasty, it is twice as high as the original statue and towers over visitors in the hall. Along both wings are 20 devas (heavenly beings) while 12 Pratyeke-Buddhas sit cross-legged behind. On the back wall is a carving depicting a young boy, Sudhana, consulting the 53 Famous Masters before attaining enlightenment. The sculpture presents 150 Buddhas of varying sizes with the Goddess of Mercy, Guanyin, in the center surrounded by Sudhana and Nagakanya, a naga maiden or daughter of the dragon king. A pair of stone pagodas, octagonal with nine stories, built in A.D. 960 by the king of Wuyue Qian Chu for Monk Yongming, stands in front of the hall.

Visitors to Lingyin Temple who can read Chinese will also be interested in visiting the halls to the left of the main buildings which house scrolls, one of which tells a popular story about the Northern Song Dynasty poet-official Su Dongpo's handling of a court case while he was governor of Hangzhou. The owner of a fan shop was accused of reneging on a 20,000 cash debt. The artisan explained that since the weather had been rainy and cold, he could not sell even a single fan. Su Dongpo asked the accused to bring him 20 fans and proceeded to write a few lines and draw a few pictures on each. Since Su Dongpo was a famous painter and calligrapher as well as a poet, the fans were quickly sold out and the debt settled.

Both Bai Juyi and Su Dongpo are known to have fre-

Statue of General Yue Fei at Yue Fei's Temple

Stone guardians at the funerary path leading to Yue Fei's Tomb

Statue of Sakyamuni at the Grand Hall, Temple of the Soul's Retreat

Stone carvings at The Peak That Flew from Afar

Temple of the Soul's Retreat

Autumn Moon on Calm Lake

Jade Spring

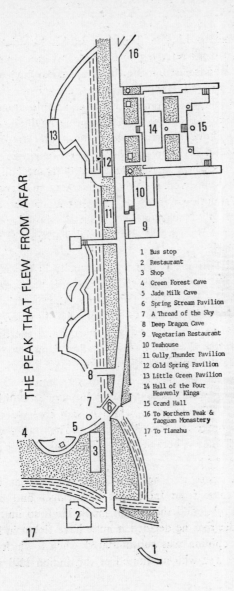

THE PEAK THAT FLEW FROM AFAR

1 Bus stop
2 Restaurant
3 Shop
4 Green Forest Cave
5 Jade Milk Cave
6 Spring Stream Pavilion
7 A Thread of the Sky
8 Deep Dragon Cave
9 Vegetarian Restaurant
10 Teahouse
11 Gully Thunder Pavilion
12 Cold Spring Pavilion
13 Little Green Pavilion
14 Hall of the Four
   Heavenly Kings
15 Grand Hall
16 To Northern Peak &
   Taoguan Monastery
17 To Tianzhu

The Temple of the Soul's Retreat Area

61

quently come to Lingyin Temple. In his "Cold Spring Pavilion", a work referring to the red and green pavilion which still stands just outside the temple, Bai Juyi wrote: "(The area around Hangzhou) offers the most beautiful scenery in southeast China. Lingyin Temple stands as the most attractive sight while Cold Spring Pavilion (*Lengquan Ting*) above everything looks most graceful." He said on another occasion that he visited Lingyin 20 times during his 600 days in the prefecture of Hangzhou. Su Dongpo also observed that during his stay in Hangzhou he made "countless visits" to Lingyin. When he served as governor of Hangzhou, he often composed poems, hosted feasts and carried out official business at Cold Spring Pavilion.

The Cold Spring Pavilion was originally in the middle of the stream but was moved to its present site right across from the Peak That Flew from Afar in the Ming Dynasty. Nearby are the Gully Thunder Pavilion (*Helei Ting*) dating from the Song Dynasty, and the Spring Stream Pavilion (*Chuncong Ting*) dating from the Ming. There are two couplets at the Cold Spring Pavilion. The first, said to be the oldest, reads in translation: "When did the spring water become cold? From where did the peak fly in?" The response which is said to have come later in the other two couplets reads: "The spring water became cold when it became cold. The peak flew in from where it flew in."

One local story also has it that the Peak That Flew from Afar came from India: the high ridges and peaks in the area reminded the Indian monk Huili so much of a hill in India that he decided it must have flown in from there. His opinion was substantiated when a black ape and a white ape who meditated at the Indian Hill were found in a cave here. Its peculiar name may also come from its being different from the hills around it. Some 209 meters high and covered with bizarre rocks and caves, it is both smaller than the surrounding hills and has a different geological structure. All the surrounding hills are made of sandstone, while the Peak That Flew from Afar is composed of limestone.

Halfway up the peak stands another pavilion, the Little Green Pavilion (*Cuiwei Ting*), which offers a good view of Lingyin Temple across the way. This pavilion is said to have been built in the Southern Song Dynasty in honor of Yue Fei by Han Shizhong, a colleague of Yue Fei who was dismissed from his post after he confronted Qin Hui, who was responsible for Yue Fei's death with the words: "How do you expect the country to accept the charge 'probably he is guilty'?"

Early records indicate that at one time there were

more than 72 caves on the Peak That Flew from Afar. The few that remain are mostly concentrated on the southeast side of the peak, including several with carvings: Green Forest Cave (*Qinglin Dong*), Jade Milk Cave (*Yuru Dong*), A Shot of Gleam Cave (*Shexu Dong*) and — near the Monk Huili Pagoda — Deep Dragon Cave

(*Longhong Dong*) where a figure of the Goddess of Mercy is carved into the rockface. This figure along with one of the Amitabha Buddha and the Mahasthamaprapta Boddhisattva on the hill's rockface are the earliest carvings, dating from the late Five Dynasties period (951). Several carvings from the Song Dynasty are on the outer rock wall of Green Forest Cave — in a stone niche the Locana Buddha sitting at the center of a lotus-flower pedestal, Manjusri Boddhisattva mounted on a lion to his left and Samantabhadra Boddhisattva on an elephant to his right along with four celestial kings and four Boddhisattva — 15 figures in all.

Other Song works include figures of 18 arhats on the rockface opposite the eastern wall of Green Forest Cave, a seated statue of Amitabha Buddha above the cave mouth as well as three Sakyamuni Buddhas and over 50 arhats on the southern wall of Jade Milk Cave. Perhaps the most famous and also the largest carving on the hill is the Song

Dynasty sculpture of the Maitreya Buddha with his round belly and smiling face.

In China, only the Dazu stone carvings in Sichuan Province can compare to the Yuan Dynasty carvings at the Peak That Flew from Afar. An example is the story carved in relief at the mouth of Deep Dragon Cave of the Tang Dynasty monk Xuanzang (Tsuantsang) on a pilgrimage to obtain Buddhist scriptures. Finely carved and well preserved, the scene shows one horse leading the way, another carrying the scriptures and a third bearing a lotus pedestal.

Taoguang Monastery (*Taoguang Si*)

Near Lingyin Temple, only a ten-minute walk through woods that give way to a bamboo forest, to the northwest is Taoguang Monastery, built in the Tang Dynasty and named after a monk-poet from Sichuan Province who was a friend of the poet-governor Bai Juyi. The two are said to have often read and composed poems together at this spot. In 1961, Taoguang Monastery was rebuilt as a large hall with a pond for golden lotuses, a rare ornamental water plant. The site offers one of the best views of the Qiantang River and can now be reached by cable cars.

Hangzhou Botanical Gardens
(*Hangzhou Zhiwuyuan*)

One of the best in China, the 500-acre (about 200 hectares) Hangzhou Botanical Gardens grow over 120 kinds of bamboo in its bamboo section, some 1,200 medicinal herbs in its Garden of a Hundred Herbs (*Baicao Yuan*), and hundreds of varieties of other trees and plants from China

and abroad including a giant sequoia redwood presented by former U.S. President Richard Nixon on his 1972 visit which opened the way towards normalization of relations between the People's Republic of China and the United States.

Even metasequoia grows here. Thought to have thrived over 100 million years ago in Europe, Asia and North America and to have become extinct over 20 million years ago, metasequoia was discovered in the 1940s growing in Sichuan and Hubei provinces in China, an event that startled botanists of the world who had only seen the tree in fossil form. Several metasequoias — with red bark, tall, straight trunks and feathery leaves — grow beside the Buttercup Pool, along with some 700 other kinds of trees and shrubs in the same plant species section. The Hangzhou Botanical Gardens' staff has also succeeded in taking cuttings from metasequoia. Other trees here include feather maple, Japanese cherry and pine, magnolia, camphor, pointy cypress, dragon cypress and pines from Mount Qomolangma.

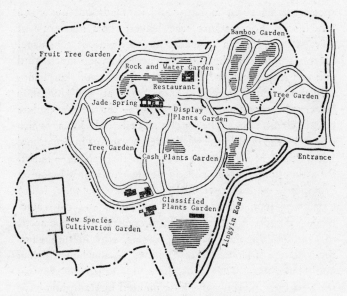

Jade Spring and Hangzhou Botanical Gardens

The bamboo, ranging in variety from a species that reaches the height of a three-storied building in a month to some that are only a few inches tall at maturity, grow in the northeast corner of the gardens, half-way along the road to Jade Spring (*Yu Quan*). Winding paths lead through the groves of bamboo including a square type and those having green, white or yellow-spotted leaves on trunks that can be green, yellow or purple and in spots or stripes which have won the name "Bamboo Kingdom" for the area.

The Garden of a Hundred Herbs is arranged in neat beds to give each herbal plant the particular kind of environment it likes to grow in. Each plant has its species' name given in Latin and its medicinal use given in Chinese. For instance, the leaves, roots and fruit of Spiraea Japonica can be made into medicine. It can dispel fever, dampness of the body, soreness from too much wind and can stop coughing. The root and leaves of the melon-seed boxwood — seen in bonsai form at the Hangzhou Flower Nursery (*Hangzhou Huapu*) — can help stimulate blood circulation. The green-leaved red lotus which flower by the pool in the garden tell a story of international friendship. More than 40 years ago their seeds — buried for a thousand years in peat in northeast China's Liaoning Province — were discovered by a Japanese botanist, Ichiro Oga, who took the seeds back to Japan and cultivated them. After the Liberation, he presented 40 of the seeds to Guo Moruo, the poet and scholar, who in turn gave them to the four cities of Beijing, Guangzhou, Wuhan and Hangzhou. The seeds, however, failed to grow in the first three places, only those planted in Hangzhou have survived and are thriving in the Botanical Gardens.

Inside the main gate, set off by trees, are various gardens with lilies, magnolias, camellia, peach and cherry trees, maple and azalea, osmanthus and myrtle. Besides the display areas, sections are also set aside for research and experimentation.

Jade Spring (*Yu Quan*)

Near Hangzhou Botanical Gardens is Jade Spring, a rectangular pool about 14 meters long, 10 meters wide and some three meters deep, surrounded by a courtyard built in 1964 at the site of a Qing Dynasty temple originally founded as a Buddhist monastery in the 5th century. The large multi-colored carp raised in the rectangular pond have attracted visitors for over 700 years while in the courtyard outside are varieties of specially-bred goldfish in large bowls.

The landscaped garden around the spring includes smaller courtyards and a pavilion in pine, bamboo and plum as well as other smaller springs and streams. The Hill-Beyond-Hill Restaurant (*Shanwaishan Caiguan*) is at Jade Spring.

Hangzhou Flower Nursery
(*Hangzhou Huapu*)

"There's a saying that boxwood will not get old even if it lives 1,000 years," said Chen Tugen, a gardener at the Hangzhou Flower Nursery as he pointed to a 100-year-old bonsai melon-seed boxwood in the Hangzhou Flower Nursery's hall of bonsai where some 50 bonsai or miniature landscapes are brought in for display each week from the hundreds grown outside. Besides a bonsai section, the nursery has three other sections — for Chinese roses, orchids and chrysanthemums — where over 2,000 flowers are cultivated.

Boxwood, five-needle pine and cypress are among the most common trees selected for the bonsai dwarfing process although any tree with a solid trunk that can withstand limited fertilizer and water and constant pruning can be used, according to Chen.

The bonsai, which are normally kept in the open air to help prevent their roots from rotting, are developed for their trunk, their leaves or their flowers and fruit depending on their variety. Some are displayed in water scenes and some grown on rocks. The pot, too, must be carefully considered to be in the right proportion. The bonsai grown at the nursery can be bought in Hangzhou at the Hangzhou Flower Shop.

Among the bonsai arranged in row after row outside stands a gnarled and twisted rock 2.6 meters high known as Rippled Cloud Peak (*Zhouyun Feng*) which is considered together with Lucky Cloud Peak in Lingering Garden at Suzhou and Exquisite Jade Peak in Yuyuan Garden at Shanghai to be the three best-known ornamental rocks in south China. According to several records, the rock was given in the late Ming and early Qing dynasties by Wu Liuqi, commander-in-chief of the army and navy divisions in Guangdong as a present to an official, Cha Yihuang, who had helped him in his youth when he was so down and out he survived by begging. The rock has changed hands several times since then and was brought to the nursery in 1963 from Chongde County northeast of Hangzhou.

Crossing a painted corridor through the Chinese Rose Garden leads to the Orchid Room where varieties of orchids are displayed in all seasons. Some of the finest here were presented by the late Marshal Zhu De (1886-1976), Chairman of the Standing Committee of the National People's Congress, who also inscribed the tablets at the entrance. One of the rarest orchids on display is known as "Green Cloud", discovered during the Qing Dynasty on Color Clouds Hill (*Wuyun Shan*) in Hangzhou. Ancient books report the cultivation of orchids in China as early as the late Spring and Autumn Period, or 2,500 years ago.

Adjoining the Orchid Room is a section for chrysanthemums where an exhibition of the best of the some 1,000 kinds cultivated is put on every autumn.

Chrysanthemums have been cultivated in Hangzhou for generations not only for their beauty but also for their tea, generally made from the white variety, and medicine, generally made from the yellow variety. As a medicinal tea, Hangzhou chrysanthemum is said to be helpful in curing colds, lowering fevers, clearing the liver, brightening the eyes, relieving poisoning and soothing inflammation. It is used to treat high blood pressure, migraine and acute conjunctivitis.

South of the Lake

Wu Hill (*Wu Shan*)

Wu Hill is actually 10 or more small peaks about 100 meters high extending into the city area and covered with interesting trees, rocks, caves, gullies and historical relics surviving from one of the oldest settled areas in Hangzhou. There is an excellent view from the top, accessible by car, especially from the Tea Bud Fragrance Hall (*Mingxiang Lou*) and the Pavilion of a Panorama View (*Jimu Ge*), now a teahouse on Precious Moon Hill (*Baoyue*

Shan) which is surrounded by ancient camphor trees from 400 to 500 years old. One of the camphors, "Song Camphor", is more than 800 years old. Retired workers from Hangzhou like to walk up the hill with their birdcages and let their pet birds learn the songs of other birds flying among the camphor, gingko, Chinese plum and other evergreens planted on top of the hill.

On the rock surface slightly below Purple Sun-Light Hill (*Ziyang Shan*) are the carved words which in translation read, "The Number One Hill," by Mi Fu, a famous calligrapher of the Song Dynasty. At the Treasure and Success Temple (*Baocheng Si*), one of the few temple sites remaining among the many here from the past, are the remains of a stone statue of the poet and monk Mahegela carved in the Yuan Dynasty. At the former site of the Three-Thatched-Hut Temple (*Sanmao Guan*) on the west-

ern slope of the Purple Sun-Light Hill is another inscription lauding a huge rock as the number one peak of Wu Hill.

A strange cluster of rocks stand north of the summit of Purple Sun-Light Hill known as the "Twelve Peaks of Witch Hill" (a pun in Chinese since the character for "witch" has the same sound as "wu" of Wu Hill). According to their different shapes, they have been given names like "Chinese writing brush holder", "incense burner", "chessboard" and "elephant's trunk". Since they also can be seen to resemble the twelve animals in the Chinese lunar calendar, the rocks are also called the "Twelve Animal Stones" (*Shi'er Shengxiao Shi*). Other rocks in curious shapes can be found beside Lucky Rock Cave (*Ruishi Dong*) on the hill.

Six Harmonies Pagoda (*Liuhe Ta*)

On the north bank of the Qiantang River stands the Six Harmonies Pagoda, first built in 970 as a nine-storied monument by Qian Chu, ruler of the Wuyue Kingdom, who hoped that besides serving as a lighthouse the structure in its magnificence would have some influence over controlling the destructive tidal waves of the Qiantang.

Burned down in 1121, the octagonal pagoda was rebuilt between 1153 and 1163 in the Southern Song Dynasty, and the brick seven-storied interior of the present-day pagoda dates back to that time. The 13-eaved wood exterior, repaired and treated for wood worms after the Liberation, last went under major restoration in 1900. Although it has been repaired many times since the Song Dynasty, the

74

structure preserves its ancient form, and in 1961 was listed by the State Council as a major site under state protection. Six harmonies, referring to the six codes of Buddhism, was originally the name of a Buddhist temple at the same site. The pagoda is also known as the Six Point Pagoda, referring to heaven and earth and the four compass points.

Viewed from a distance, the 59.89-meter-high pagoda stands out not only because of its impressive size but also because of the distinct layered effect created by the eaves — light on top and dark underneath — a traditional Chinese architectural technique of alternating light and shade to enhance a view from a distance.

Inside the pagoda on the ceiling of each story are carved and painted figures of flowers, birds and animals while outside on the corner of each eave hang bells and slates to keep live birds from nesting. Visitors may climb to the top up a steep spiral staircase, pausing at each story to

look out over the countryside and the view of the hills, fields, the town of Xiaoshan across the river and, perhaps, a train crossing the 1,453-meter-long Qiantang Bridge, built in 1934-37 for both rail and road traffic as the first modern bridge designed and built by Chinese engineers and workers. Nearby the pagoda is the Exhibition Hall of the Martyr Cai Yongxiang, a People's Liberation Army soldier who died when he removed a piece of log from the bridge rail in 1966.

For centuries, the Six Harmonies Pagoda has provided a special vantage point for viewing the Qiantang River which is known for a rare and spectacular sight that happens every fall, a tidal wave or "bore". This phenomenon — usually at its height around the autumnal equinox in late September — traditionally attracts visitors to Hangzhou for "viewing the bore". Actually, the best site for viewing the bore has changed over the years. From the Ming Dynasty until around 1949, the best place to see it was at the town of Yanguan in Haining County, some 48 kilometers east of Hangzhou. After that, river

works and land reclamation caused the bore to shift with the course of the river. Today, the river course has taken its main thrust back to Haining although the bore can also be seen in Hangzhou.

Rising on the borders between Zhejiang, Jiangxi and Anhui provinces, the Qiantang River travels some 410 kilometers across Zhejiang Province until it reaches the sea near Hangzhou. The trumpet-shape of the river — 100 kilometers wide at Hangzhou Bay narrowing to only three kilometers at Haining — and the pull of the tide creates a bore so powerful it can carry massive boulders in its wake. Early in this century, Frederick Cloud, an American consular official in China, who wrote a guidebook to Hangzhou, described the sound of the bore's arrival: "The roar is deafening and may be likened to the roar of the great Niagara."

Depending on tidal currents and prevailing winds, the crested-wall of water reaches heights varying from six to 20 feet. Today the bore, which caused flooding for hundreds of years, has been brought under control by dams and stone embankments. In more recent years, extensive river work has enabled some 155,000 acres (about 62,000 hectares) of tideland to be reclaimed for cultivation that had previously been flooded by the bore.

The phenomenon of the bore has also given rise to legends, including that of the god of the bore, Wu Zixu. It is said that a court advisor, Wu Zixu was ordered to commit suicide after warning the King of Wu in the Spring and Autumn Period to be prepared against counterattacks by the defeated Kingdom of Yue. About to die, Wu Zixu asked that his eyes be hung on the south gate of the capital so he could see Yue defeat Wu. Angered, the King of Wu ordered Wu Zixu's corpse wrapped in a leather case and thrown into the Qiantang River. From then on, according to the legend, there was a bore and Wu Zixu became the god of the river bore.

There are records of Gou Jian (?-465 B.C.) King of Yue commenting on the momentum of the bore, which can be heard on its way a halfhour before its arrival. And *Records of the Historian* reports that when the First Emperor of Qin (259-210 B.C.) arrived at the Qiantang River, the turbulent water forced him to turn westward 120 kilometers to cross the river at a narrower point on his way to Shaoxing, southeast of Hangzhou. Another story tells of the shock the river bore caused Emperor Zhao Gou (1107-87) of Southern Song. Having fled to Hangzhou from the north, he was spending the night at Wave Sound Temple (*Chaoming Si*) when the sound of the river bore not only woke him up but made him think the Jin troops had caught up with him.

During the Southern Song Dynasty, "viewing the bore" in the eighth lunar month became regarded as a festival, a custom carried on through to the Yuan, Ming and Qing times. According to historic record, at the time of the Song Dynasty, public figures from Hangzhou started their festivities about the 11th and continued until the 20th of the eighth month with the height of the festival on the 18th known as the "Bore's Birthday". This was also the day for the court to review the navy. Stands for the wealthy were put up stretching for over a dozen kilometers along the river in the area of the Six Harmonies Pagoda. First came the naval drill with live amunition. At the point of the highest tide, the prefecture governor presented a sacrifice to the god of the tide. Several hundred tattooed swimming champions dived into the river heading towards the roaring head of the bore. Some held large colored flags or carried gaudy parasols. Others rolled logs with their legs or performed other stunts as they swam.

Today's "viewing of the bore" is not nearly as lavish, but the bore does come to Hangzhou around the time of Mid-Autumn Festival (the 15th day of the eighth lunar month), and crowds still line the river to watch the bore come thundering through.

Clouds Lingering (*Yunqi*)

Not too far west from Six Harmonies Pagoda is an area known as Clouds Lingering (*Yunqi*) where a foot-path leads one kilometer along a stream through a tall green bamboo forest. Aside from its scenic value, the bamboo woods at Clouds Lingering provide more than 3,000 Moso bamboo poles for park construction in China every year. Other characteristic vegetation of sub-tropical areas grows here, too, including a 38-meter-high Chinese sweet gum tree almost 1,000 years old. Just east of Clouds Lingering is another good hike up Color Clouds Hill (*Wuyun Shan*) which at 344.7 meters is the third highest hill in the West Lake area. At the top are three old wells and a 1,000-year-old gingko tree with a circumference at its base which takes five people to join hands around it.

Nine Creeks and Eighteen Gullies (*Jiuxi Shibajian*)

Another ideal place to go walking in the west hills in the same area is Nine Creeks and Eighteen Gullies which has a path going down the hill from Dragon Well (*Long-jing*) that twists and turns some seven kilometers down hill — crossing and recrossing a stream — until it comes out near the Qiantang River at a point not far from the Six Harmonies Pagoda. There is a restaurant by the stream half-way down. According to the late geologist Li Siguang, the steep topography here was created during the Quaternary Period (from 10,000 to three million years ago) when West Lake was a frozen expanse of ice and snow and glaciers slid across the area — marked by glacial stratification — towards the southeast.

Tiger Spring (*Hupao*)

The clear quality of the water at Tiger Spring, also known as Running Tiger Spring, has earned it the ranking of the "third spring in the country" behind Jade Spring at Beijing and Cold Spring at Jinshan Temple in Zhenjiang — and the reputation for being the best place in Hangzhou to drink Dragon Well tea.

The thing to do, then, at Tiger Spring — after walking up from the road about a kilometer through a pine and bamboo forest to the renovated temple complex that surrounds it — is to relax with a cup of tea made from what the local people call "the two uniques" — Dragon Well tea and Tiger Spring water.

"If you came to this place without trying the tea and water, you wouldn't have been here," said He Qi, over a cup of tea further complimented by a sesame sweet crisp available from the concession.

Besides tasting the water, visitors can test it — through an experiment of dropping coins into a bowl filled with Tiger Spring water that shows its high molecular density. Filled to the brim and beyond, the water will rise some two to three millimeters above the edge without overflowing because of its high surface tension to form an unusually high meniscus. Filtered through the quartz and sandstone of the surrounding hills, the water is also said to be bacteria free.

Originally built in 819 A.D. in the Tang Dynasty, the temple was reconstructed and enlarged on several occasions from 1862 to 1908 during the Qing Dynasty. One of the well-known personages associated with the temple is Li Shutong, a master calligrapher and painter, who gave his seals to the Xiling Seal-Engraving Society when he became monk Hongyi and came to live here in 1918.

According to the legend which gives the site its name, there was not always water at Tiger Spring. Xingkong, the Tang Dynasty monk who founded the temple, had almost decided to move to a new site because of lack of drinking water. However, one night he had a dream in which he was told that soon two tigers would come to his aid. They arrived the next day, running to claw the ground and open the spring to provide the water which today is bottled and sold on domestic and foreign market as Chrysanthemum Brand Mineral Water.

Hangzhou Zoo (*Hangzhou Dongwuyuan*)

The goldfish aquarium to the east of the main gate of the Hangzhou Zoo displays in glass tanks set in the wall of its corridors some of the most unusual and rare goldfish that can be seen in China — Red Bubble, Purple Crown, Silver Lion Head, Black Dragon Eyes — exotic names to describe the exotic colors and shapes of these fish bred since ancient times in China, and particularly in Hangzhou which is one of the places the art of raising goldfish originated.

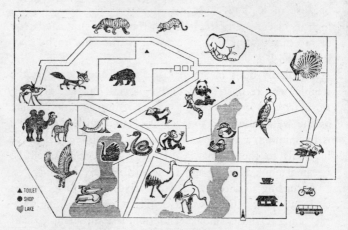

Hangzhou Zoo

Goldfish or "brocade" fish evolved from the golden carp which we know were cultivated in Hangzhou as long as 900 years ago when Su Dongpo wrote poems about them. From the early Yuan Dynasty, when they began to be raised in basins or bowls, more varieties were developed and by Ming times cultivation of goldfish had become a popular hobby. Since the Liberation, the number of species raised in Hangzhou has increased to more than 100. Hangzhou goldfish are now sold not only in other parts of China

A snapshot of West Lake

Dragon
Well

A bamboo
path at
Clouds
Lingering.

Six Harmonies Pagoda

Viewing
Fish at
Flower Harbor

"*Shuizhuju*" — a
corner of the West
Lake Guesthouse

but also exported.

Adjoining Tiger Spring, the Hangzhou Zoo provides a home for its many species of animals from both China and abroad in a park setting that ranges up along the side of Grand Benevolence Hill (*Daci Shan*) south of West Lake, taking advantage of the hill's natural features to create an ecological environment suited to the animals' particular living habits and characteristics. Besides the goldfish aquarium, the zoo includes song-bird and wild bird aviaries, a snake house, panda house, small animal garden, park for grassland animals, bear and monkey hills, tiger mountain, leopard house, lion house, sea-lion pond, water-fowl lake and mandarin duck pond.

Dragon Well (*Longjing*)

The Dragon Well for which the famous green tea is named is located at a small temple converted into a teahouse in a beautiful grove of bamboo and pine and masses of wisteria on Fenghuang Ridge (*Fenghuang Ling*).

It is one and a half kilometers from Dragon Well village in the rolling hills west of West Lake.

Actually, there are four varieties of Dragon Well tea named Lion, Dragon, Cloud and Tiger after the peaks in the area on which they are grown: Lion Peak (*Shi Feng*), Dragon Well, Clouds Lingering and Tiger Spring. Of them,

"Lion Peak Dragon Well tea" is said to be the best. But tourists should be advised that although the best-grade Dragon Well tea is served at the teahouses, it is not sold locally by bulk because the best grade tea is bought by the state for distribution elsewhere in China and for export. Good loose green tea can be bought in boxes at the Dragon Well concession, as well as at other teahouses, while the real — and expensive — Dragon Well tea can be bought at the Friendship Store in Hangzhou.

The Dragon Well itself is a circular pond formed by a spring. The water gushes out from a rockface to collect in the well and flow on through cracks in the rocks to two small, interconnected square ponds, from where it drains once again into a larger pond and down to a brook at the foot of the ridge. The murmuring of these streams and brooks adds to the beauty of the place. The water in Dragon Well has the special feature, created by two levels of springs that feed it, that when its water is disturbed instead of concentric circles a line appears on the surface like a hair spring. Behind the well stands "The Rock Sent by Immortals" (*Shenyun Shi*), about two meters high which is said to resemble a dragon at play and which records say was fished out of the well by a military officer in 1448 in the Ming Dynasty.

The Dragon Well Temple (*Longjing Si*) was originally built in A.D. 949 during the Five Dynasties Period at a site half a kilometer away and was moved to its present location in 1438 in the Ming Dynasty. People like to come here on a summer day to chat, sitting about in wicker chairs over tea and lotus root porridge mixed with osmanthus blossoms.

"Old people stay all day but young people get restless after a couple of hours," explained one Hangzhou resident during a recent visit.

The old people may be entertaining themselves by exchanging stories about the history of the place, including how the nearby Pavilion of Going Beyond the Brook (*Guoxi Ting*) below Fenghuang Ridge got its name:

It seems that in the Northern Song Dynasty a monk named Biancai lived at the temple who, claiming old age as an excuse, never saw his guests off further than the nearby stream. When Su Dongpo was an official at Hangzhou, he heard of the monk and made a special trip to Dragon Well to see him, staying overnight at the temple. The next day, Biancai saw him off and, since they were having a very interesting talk together, forgot himself and accompanied Su Dongpo across the bridge. When this was pointed out to him, the old monk smiled and quoted these lines from classical poetry:

"You and I make a pair of old men,
It's pleasant to keep each other's company."

From then on, the bridge was called Going Beyond the
Brook Bridge (*Guoxi Qiao*), and the pavilion which stands
there today was built to commemorate the event.

Some visitors may want to stop by Dragon Well for
a cup of tea after or before a visit to the nearby Three
Caves at Yanxia (*Yanxia Sandong*).

Three Caves at Yanxia
(*Yanxia Sandong*)

Two of the most exquisite stone carvings in Hangzhou
stand at the entrance of the Haze at Sunset Cave (*Yanxia
Dong*), the highest and oldest (discovered in A.D. 10th
century) of the three caves at Yanxia Ridge situated along
a new and beautifully landscaped highway a short distance
from Dragon Well. The other caves further down the
road are Water Music Cave (*Shuile Dong*) and Stone
House Cave (*Shiwu Dong*).

Both sculptures — the Guanyin or Goddess of Mercy to
the left on entering the Haze at Sunset Cave and the
Mahasthamaprapta Boddhisattva on the right — were
carved in the early Song Dynasty, while some 20 sculptures within the cave itself date from the Five Dynasties.
The Guanyin is particularly interesting for the bold presentation of her as a secular beauty, one shoulder lower
than the other with her hands gracefully crossed in front.
This statue — as did others in the cave — suffered minor
damage during the "cultural revolution" when its nose

was broken. But staff from the Hangzhou Parks Administration were able to prevent the major destruction suffered during that period by the more accessible and open Stone House Cave, by bricking in the entrance of Haze at Sunset Cave. The cave is said to have gotten

its name from the view at sunset with the smoke rising from the chimneys from Manjuelong Village just below. A walk from Haze at Sunset Cave up the south peak leads to the largest cave in Hangzhou, Thousand Men's Cave which is 300 meters long.

Water Music Cave is located just west of Manjuelong Village and the path to it from the highway leads through the front yard of one of the homes in the village through a grove of osmanthus trees. Marble-topped tables provide a good place to picnic outside the entrance to this 60-meter-long cave which receives its name from the gurgling sound of a spring at the entrance echoing throughout the cave.

The site of Stone House

Cave at the bottom of the hill, with its surrounding garden, pavilion and teahouse, underwent major renovation in 1980. During the "cultural revolution", the 516 carvings of Buddhas on the wall of the 5.6-meter-high main cave — an airy room on the side of the hill — were smashed. Rather than leave them in a grotesque condition, the Hangzhou Parks Administration sanded them down and their traces, literally shadows of their former selves, can be seen. The cave and its carvings date back to the Late Jin of the Five Dynasties.

Another attraction of a trip to the Three Caves at Yanxia in the fall is the osmanthus which blooms all along the hill and particularly in and around the Manjuelong Village at the foot of the hill, filling the whole valley with their fragrance.

And if the fragrance is not enough, osmanthus can be eaten in the form of a sweet glace or a thick soup made with the blossoms and chestnuts or drunk in the form of osmanthus flower wine.

Jade Emperor Hill and Phoenix Hill
(*Yuhuang Shan*, *Fenghuang Shan*)

At the top of Jade Emperor Hill (*Yuhuang Shan*) is a view of Hangzhou on one side and the Qiantang River on the other from a renovated temple, now a restaurant and teahouse, which was originally built as a Buddhist temple and rebuilt as a Taoist temple during the Qing Dynasty. The well at the site, with its white jadestone rail, dates from the Song Dynasty. The 239-meter-high summit can be reached by walking or by a 4.23-kilometer-long road which winds its way 2.5 times around the hill to the top. Halfway up is Purple Source Cave (*Zilai Dong*) which has another deep cave inside and can hold about 200 people. From this point on the road, it is possible to look down on the fields below to see the remains of a field in the shape of an octagon that is said to have been tend-

ed by the emperor himself during the Southern Song Dynasty.

In 1963, a star chart carved in red sandstone, 4.71 meters long, 2.66 meters wide and 0.31 meters thick, was discovered at the foot of Jade Emperor Hill at the grave of Qian Yuanguan, King of the Wuyue Kingdom of the Five Dynasties. Considered to be the oldest such chart in the world, the stone is believed to have been carved before the king's burial ceremony in February 942, which took place six months after the king's death in August the previous year. It therefore is some 300 years earlier than the Suzhou star chart carved in 1247 which had been regarded throughout the world as the oldest of its kind. The stone is kept in the Temple of Confucius on Laodong Road, Hangzhou.

Phoenix Hill (*Fenghuang Shan*), close to Jade Emperor Hill, was the site of the prefectural government during the Tang Dynasty and the capital of the Wuyue Kingdom during the Five Dynasties. Although no traces of its former splendor remain, the Southern Song imperial court and gardens replete with palace — some 80 or 90 of them — as well as numerous other courtyards and pavilions were built here.

To the south of Phoenix Hill is a stone niche — four meters high and 9.7 meters wide — with carved Buddhas dating from the Late Jin of the Five Dynasties. The three

sitting Buddhas — Amitabha, Guanyin, and Mahasthama-prapta Boddhisattva — are among the oldest rock-cave carvings at West Lake. Outside the gate of Fantian Temple (*Fantian Si*) at Phoenix Hill stand pillars with Buddhist inscriptions dating them back more than 1,000 years.

Meijiawu Village (*Meijiawu Cun*)
(Tea Production Brigade)

Sipping a cup of the Meijiawu Brigade's first-grade Dragon Well tea, Chen Wuyun, the 59-year-old leader of Meijiawu Brigade, West Lake People's Commune, placed one of the tiny loose green tea leaves in front of her on the mahogany table.

"This Dragon Well tea has four special characteristics," she said. "It has a good green color, it's fragrant, it has a good refreshing flavor, and it contains one spear and one broad leaf — that's how the leaves are picked and how they keep their shape."

These characteristics have helped make Dragon Well tea — produced in the Hangzhou area for over 1,000 years — one of the most famous varieties in China.

It was a cold morning in January 1982 — the coldest of the year according to Chen Wuyun, and the first cup of tea was followed by a second (considered the best by tea-drinking connoisseurs) and a third as Chen Wuyun talked about the history and production of tea at the brigade which lies in a valley surrounded by hills of tea plants some 12 kilometers from Hangzhou.

The road to the commune leads past the Chinese Academy of Sciences' Tea Research Institute before reaching the village of some 350 households which in 1981 produced over 125 metric tons of tea.

The signs of prosperity evident all over the West Lake area are here, for example, in the bricks laid out for construction of a new store. Besides 75 hectares of tea plants, the brigade also plants five hectares of rice and manages a tea processing plant and several small factories producing quilt covers, embroidery and furniture.

In the brigade's meeting room with its mahogany furniture formerly owned by the landlords, Chen Wuyun explained that the average wage of a laborer is now 74 yuan a month, a salary that closes the gap between what farm workers and factory workers make to the degree that the brigade's young women, who used to look for more prosperous husbands in the city, are choosing to stay in the village to marry.

"Before the Liberation, tea growers did not have enough to eat although they worked all year round. Since 1952, our place has gradually taken on the road of collective farming and, especially in recent years, we've had a great increase in tea and agricultural output," said Chen Wuyun.

The Meijiawu Brigade's development in its early days (At the time of the Liberation in 1949, the brigade cultivated 40 hectares of land, producing 18,000 kilograms of tea a year) was greatly encouraged by the late Premier Zhou Enlai who made five visits to the brigade between 1957 and 1963. On the wall of the meeting room hangs an award of merit — one among many honors from both home and abroad presented to the brigade — signed by Premier Zhou Enlai himself.

"Zhou Enlai was very dear to the people here. After our meetings, for example, he would visit the homes and make minute inquiries, asking how many members there

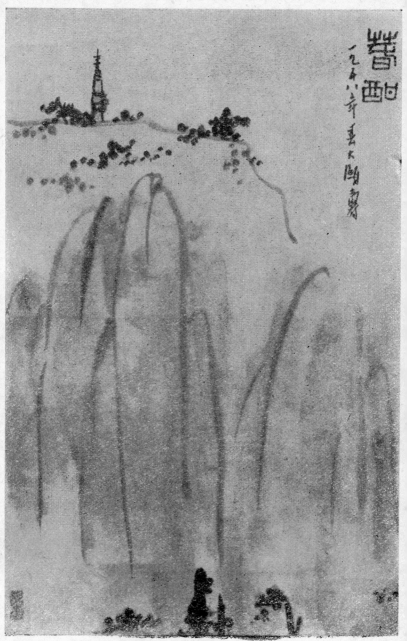

Spring Dream by Pan Tianshou

were in the family, what they were eating, what they ate that day, how many pigs they kept and how many they sold to the state or kept for themselves," Chen Wuyun said.

Many other prominent people, including the American author Edgar Snow, came to see this center of tea production which dates back over 1,000 years. Tea is still picked by hand, mostly by women, and roasted in open bins that were converted to electricity from wood-burning in the early 1960s.

"To pick tea takes a concentrated mind, sharp eyes and quick hands," said Chen Wuyun, who herself con-

"Also marvelous in rain" — a line of poetry by Su Dongpo to describe West Lake. by Li Keran

tinues to spend a considerable amount of time working in the fields along with her administrative responsibilities as brigade leader.

An energetic and bright-eyed woman, Chen Wuyun seems living proof of her claims for the benefits of drinking tea. "It's rich in chlorophyll and vitamin C. Generally good for the health, it especially helps the eyes and the brain. It helps blood circulation and digestion and helps solve the problem of overweight."

Chen Wuyun said that tea-picking was revolutionized in the early 1959 by one worker in the brigade, Shen Shunzhao, now 45 and still a "model worker", who introduced a method of picking tea with both hands instead of one.

"She used to go up into the hills and pick tree leaves and by this practice developed her skill. With her in the lead, now many people use two hands and can pick from 50-69 kilograms a day while before it was a maximum of 10 kilograms," Chen Wuyun said.

The timing of the tea picking is also extremely important, there being four different seasons, from the end of March until the 20th of October, for picking tea which affects the tea's grade or quality.

The finest tea is picked just as the leaf tips are beginning to show and is known as "Lotus Seed Tea". Most skilled tea-pickers can pick only 12 ounces a day and it takes two kilograms of green tea leaves to produce only half a kilogram of dry roasted tea.

Speed is very important and during the agricultural season commune members may work over 10 hours a day. They have a saying: "Three days earlier, it's a precious thing; three days later, it's useless grass."

The tea picked by mid-April when the tea buds are longer and tea stems are in leaves is called second spring tea or "Banner and Spear Tea" because the leaf looks like a banner and the long, thin bud like a spear. The third spring tea is picked early in May when the buds are large. About a month later the fourth spring tea is picked which is known as "Sparrow Tongue Tea" because its two full-sized leaves are in the shape of sparrow tongues.

Historical records, such as the works of Bai Juyi, show that as early as the Tang Dynasty tea from this area was an important commercial item. For instance, it was used as barter with areas in Xinjiang and Mongolia for horses in an exchange called "Tea and Horse Policy".

Today the brigade contracts with the state to produce a certain amount of tea each year. Before 1978, the state bought all the tea no matter how much the commune produced. Under the new economic policies — which have also raised the state purchasing prices for agricultural produce — if the target amount is exceeded the brigade can either sell the excess to the state at a higher price or take it to another market. In 1981, the brigade exceeded its 125-metric-ton target by 3,000 kilograms which was both sold to the state at higher prices and made into jasmine tea to be sold at local shops.

"Our progress is good but it's a far cry from the more advanced production brigades. We depend heavily on manual labor — hands to pick tea and to pull carts," said Chen Wuyun.

Still, there is "no comparison" between life in the village today and before the Liberation. In her own case, for instance, comparing her life and that of her parents, Chen Wuyun said that when she was 14 her father, who gathered firewood in the hills to support his wife and three daughters, died after suffering a bad fall which damaged his bladder.

The Qiantang River by Fu Baoshi

"We had no money for a doctor," she said.

Chen Wuyun said shortly after her father's death her mother gave birth to another child which had to be sold since there was no way of taking care of her.

"My first sister was sent away to work as a maid for a wealthy family and my other sister, who was four, was given away." This sister was so badly mistreated that she gradually lost her sight from malnutrition, and Chen Wuyun's mother decided that if they were going to die, they would "all die together", and brought her sister home. The family lived on begging and through the help of herbal medicine, her sister's eyesight returned. Both sisters and her mother are alive and well today, but the infant who was sold has never been found.

"Of course, this was not only the situation in my family but for most poor people. Now we are enjoying a much better life, but we shouldn't forget. . . ."

Today most of the medical costs of villagers are covered by the brigade which also runs a school for 140 students and a nursery and kindergarten to care for children of women who are working in the fields.

Besides entertaining visitors from all over the world — another presentation made to the brigade, a brocade flag presented in the winter of 1978 by a delegation of overseas Chinese from Hawaii reads: "Although we live in Honolulu, our hearts are in our home-country" — Mei-jiawu sends its tea experts to help other tea-producing areas both in China and abroad. The former head of the production brigade, Sun Guanshun, has several times gone to the Republic of Guinea to help with that country's tea development.

In the City

Listening to Orioles Singing
in the Willows (*Liulang Wenying*)
(One of the "Ten Views")

One of the first places to notice that spring has arrived in Hangzhou is among the green weeping willows which line the one-kilometer-long granite lake-front walk at Listening to Orioles Singing in the Willows Park. Birds do sing here, too, including those brought in cages by elderly citizens of Hangzhou who enjoy coming early (the 50-acre or 20-hectare park opens at 5 a.m.) for a cup of tea with friends at Listening to Orioles Singing Hall (*Wenying Guan*) with its interconnecting pavilions and corridors and wide view of the park. Before the Liberation, Listening to Orioles Singing in the Willows was a neglected tract of land overgrown with weeds around King Qian's Temple (*Qianwang Ci*), originally built for Qian Liu (852-932), king of the Five Dynasties' Wuyue Kingdom which had Hangzhou as its capital. Today the temple has been converted into an indoor garden with springs, pavilions and terraced trees and flowers. The Steles of Loyalty (*Biaozhong Bei*) at the temple were carved in the middle of the Ming Dynasty by the governor of Hangzhou, Chen Ke. Among the willows and evergreens, the spring seasonals at the park — like oriental cherry, cedar, crabapple, peach, magnolia, hydrangea and Chinese rose — offer a magnificent sight in spring although probably not as magnificent as that offered by the original Song Dynasty Garden of Scenery (*Jujing Yuan*) built at this location for the emperor and high officials. It is recorded as having been the most magnificent of several

royal gardens built around West Lake in that era. Next to Listening to Orioles Singing Hall in a grove of cherry trees stands a yellow granite memorial erected in 1963 jointly by the people of Hangzhou and of Gifu in Japan. The inscription inlaid with gold in the calligraphy of Gifu Mayor Matsuo Gosaku reads: "Japan and China will not fight again."

Listening to Orioles Singing in the Willows is a traditional site to celebrate the West Lake Lantern Festival which comes shortly after Spring Festival. Lanterns, both traditional and modern, are floated on the lake with candles and displayed in the garden.

Adjoining Listening to Orioles Singing in the Willows is Golden Ox Emerging Park (*Yongjin Gongyuan*), 2.5 kilometers along the lake, which includes a children's playground equipped with an elephant slide, electric windmill and plane, a photo-electric shooting range and jungle gyms. Boat rides are also available here.

Lakeside Park (*Hubin Gongyuan*)

One of the most popular places to come in the early morning to practice shadow-boxing, *Taiji Quan,* the gardens of Lakeside Park stretch about one kilometer along the east bank of West Lake. From 1648 until 1911, this area was closed to the public as a part of the Qing "Banner Camp" military garrison surrounded by a 20-foot-high wall 4.5 kilometers in circumference. After the Revolution of 1911, the wall was torn down and the site reopened. The largest of several gardens in the park is the First Garden in the south where the main boating quay is located. In the Sixth Garden to the north is the statue of a fighter in the Chinese People's Volunteer Army. Lakeside Park is also a good place to come in the evening to watch the sunset over the lake and the hills beyond.

Phoenix Mosque (*Fenghuang Si*)

The Phoenix Mosque on Zhongshang Road (Middle Section) in Hangzhou is one of the major Islamic mosques in China with stone carvings in Arabic. Built in the Tang Dynasty and repaired in the Ming Dynasty, the mosque was most recently restored in 1953. The Great Hall, the oldest building on the site, has three thrones of dark sandstone from the Song Dynasty. The carvings from the Koran on the middle throne are said to have been done in 1451 when the mosque was rebuilt in the Ming Dynasty.

Hangzhou Silk and
Other Handicrafts

Hangzhou Silk

With its many restaurants and shops, downtown Hangzhou is a good city to walk around in along streets lined by plane trees and bustling with people. Those interested in picking up a souvenir along the way can choose from a variety of locally produced handicrafts which, besides being available at local retail and department stores, can be found at the City Arts and Crafts Store on Yan'an Road, the Provincial Arts and Crafts Store at the Zhejiang Exhibition Hall, the shop at the Hangzhou Hotel and the Light-Industry Fair adjacent to the hotel, and the Friendship Store. Products on the market include: carvings of stone, bamboo, ivory, shell, wood and jade; clay sculptures; bone and wood inlay; gold and silver jewelry; woven bamboo animals, screens and baskets; lace; embroidery; parasols; bamboo, bone and sandlewood fans; bamboo chopsticks and walking sticks; Chinese brushes and inks; Zhang Xiaoquan scissors, and, of course, silk.

As the capital of Zhejiang Province — which produces one-third of China's raw silk, brocade, and satin — Hangzhou is one of the silk capitals of the world, and has been since ancient times. The Hangzhou Silk Printing and Dyeing Complex at Gongchen Bridge near the Grand Canal is the largest such complex in China, employing 5,800 people engaged in all the industrial processes of making silk, from unraveling cocoons to sewing the finished printed and woven materials into clothes for the domestic and world market. While many processes are now automated, pulling the thread from the cocoon is still done by hand to ensure its quality — just one of the reasons silk is expensive. The second is the complex and risky agricultural process involved in the growing of mulberry trees and raising of silk worms. And another reason, of course, is the quality of the "queen of fabrics" itself — light, soft, durable and beautiful.

Recently, the Hangzhou Silk Printing and Dyeing Complex, which was established in 1960, has revived the traditional craft of hand-printed designs and has made trial runs of silk for Japanese and other styles of clothing, scarves, quilt covers and skirt material.

The Hangzhou Silk Printing and Dyeing Complex is one of 273 silk factories employing some 90,000 workers operating under the Zhejiang Provincial Silk Corporation.

One-third of Zhejiang Province's silk goes abroad, primarily to Hongkong, France, Italy and Japan. In 1980, the province was permitted under new economic policies to deal directly in foreign trade, which is bringing more buyers from other countries, like the United States and West Germany, to Hangzhou. Meanwhile, the Zhejiang Provincial Silk Corporation is experimenting with colors, designs and patterns for the foreign market.

In China itself, most silk is sold as material, rather than as ready-made clothes. Interestingly, one-third of all Zhejiang silk distributed in China goes to minority nationalities, primarily residing in Inner Mongolia and Tibet

棲霞嶺下開桃漫
興寫此
九十四叟黃賓虹

At the foot of **Qixia Ridge** (traditional Chinese painting) by Huang Binhong

Three Pools Mirroring the Moon (traditional Chinese painting) by Tong Zhongtao

Xiling Seal-
Engraving
Society

Daybreak   at
Solitary   Hill

A View of Baochu Pagoda in the distance

autonomous regions. Many people there like its functional quality of keeping them warm without collecting dust.

The Hangzhou Brocade Factory, established in 1922, is another silk factory to visit in Hangzhou, known for its machine-made brocade pictures of scenic places in China and abroad. Especially popular in Japan and southeast Asian markets, silk handicraft articles in brocade include bedspreads, carpets and cushions.

The tradition of creating works of art in silk dates to the Song Dynasty when local Hangzhou authorities set up a department for the manufacture of silk products. An example of Southern Song brocade art can be seen in the Palace Museum in Beijing.

West Lake Silk Parasols

Frames of West Lake silk parasols are made from a particular kind of bamboo found only in Zhejiang Province which is moderately thick with a bright luster; its stem is strong enough to withstand even the hottest weather. One branch from this bamboo is split into 32 or 36 strips and a handle is added to complete the framework. When a silk parasol is shut, the silk is folded inside and the bamboo frame forms into a section of round bamboo. Zhu Zhen-fei, a craftsman at the Hangzhou Research Institute for Handicraft Arts and one of the area's first parasol makers, recalls that the early silk parasols, first produced in 1933, were rather crude and favored drab colors. The covering of today's parasols is made of light, stretched silk that comes in many different designs and colors.

Hangzhou Fans

Wu Zimu, the Southern Song writer, noted that in the Southern Song Dynasty the trading that went on day and night in the streets of Hangzhou included "painted silk fans, colored paper fans, fans with flower silhouettes ... and scented fans". Some 700 or 800 years later, the assortment of Hangzhou fans today is even greater in ten main categories: black paper fans, white paper fans, bone fans, dark bamboo fans, round palace fans, ivory fans, sandalwood fans, stage prop fans, feather fans and light fans.

Perhaps the best known fans produced at the Wang Xingji Fan Factory, which was first established in 1875 during the Qing Dynasty and produces some six million fans a year, are the black paper fans and the sandalwood fans. The large black paper fan with its covering of high-grade cotton paper coated on both sides with several layers of a special paint made from persimmon juice has been called a "mini-umbrella". The sandalwood fans give forth scents such as rose and snow-pear which last as long as the fan itself.

Hangzhou fans are often painted or inscribed. Wang Xingji Fan Factory makes a kind of fan decorated in bold calligraphy with 100 different old-style characters for the word "longevity". Another type of black paper fan has more than 40 famous poems, both ancient and modern, praising West Lake in real gold lettering with some 1,300 characters written on the fan's surface. In recent years, artists from the Shanghai Academy of Chinese Paintings and the Zhejiang Fine Arts Institute have frequently worked on decorating Hangzhou fans.

Zhang Xiaoquan Scissors

"The scissors don't cut and things are a mess", said Li Yu, a ruler of Southern Tang (10th century) in one of his poems. Someone later suggested that if he had had a pair of Zhang Xiaoquan scissors on him things would have been better. Zhang Xiaoquan Scissors Factory produces some nine million pairs of scissors a year, many the distinctive large-loop-handled ones. Besides being handsome, they are sharp: At a conference in 1978 to evaluate scissors produced at factories around the province, a pair of the large size Zhang Xiaoquan household scissors cut through 50 layers of thin white cloth, snipping cleanly through the first time.

Zhang Xiaoquan scissors date back to a Ming Dynasty craftsman. One story has it that the Qing Emperor Qianlong bought a pair of Zhang Xiaoquan scissors on a visit to Hangzhou and afterward sent people to Hangzhou every year to buy large numbers of the scissors for use in the palace. Today the line of scissors manufactured includes household scissors, scissors for cutting cloth, scissors for industrial use, scissors for embroidery and handicrafts, scissors for surgical use, shears and secateurs used in animal husbandry and agriculture. Some souvenir pairs are engraved with West Lake scenes and other patterns.

Tianzhu Chopsticks

Tianzhu chopsticks are made of bamboo with one end capped in silver, ivory, bone or pearl. Pictures are scorched into the body of the chopstick with designs on traditional Chinese themes as well as scenes of West Lake.

The manufacture of West Lake Tianzhu chopsticks began during the Qing Dynasty under the reign of Emperor Guangxu (r. 1875-1908). A story has it that there was a tea-grower from Tianzhu who found he had forgotten to bring along his chopsticks for lunch. Noticing that the hill was covered with small bamboo, he cut himself a pair to eat with and from then on, the peasants in the area of Tianzhu and Lingyin made chopsticks from the bamboo on the hill.

Restaurant Guide

Hangzhou offers a wide range of excellent restaurants. Four of the better known ones (followed by a list of other recommended restaurants) are:

Louwailou (Building Beyond Building) Restaurant

The elegant Louwailou Restaurant stands under a grey tile roof with traditional upturned eaves between the Su and Bai causeways on Solitary Hill Island to offer visitors not only delicacies of Hangzhou style cooking, but also an excellent view of the West Lake through its modern pane glass windows.

Renovated in 1980 to conform with national architectural style and the surrounding scenery, Louwailou Restaurant goes back over 130 years. Its name is commonly believed to have derived, together with that of Shanwaishan (Hill Beyong Hill) Restaurant located at Jade Spring, from a line of poetry written by Southern Song poet Lin Sheng to describe the Hangzhou scenery. Some people, however, believe another story: After the restaurant was built, the proprietor asked a reputed scholar to name his enterprise for him. The scholar said off-handedly: "Since your restaurant is next to my home, let's call it Building Beyond Building."

The restaurant's menu of some 20 traditional Hang-zhou dishes and more than 100 other delicacies is topped by West Lake Vinegar Fish. Said to have been the creation of a Su Causeway resident in the Ming Dynasty, the sweet-and-sour dish is prepared from West Lake carp of about half a kilogram in weight which is first kept in a special tank for a day or two to remove any smell of mud from the lake bottom-dwelling fish.

When he visited the restaurant for the ninth and also the last time of his life on September 16, 1973, the late Premier Zhou Enlai gave specific instructions on the planned renovations of the building which were begun in 1978 and completed two years later.

The present 3,700-square-meter restaurant, three times larger than the original, provides six dining halls on two stories to seat over 1,000 people at a time. A shop on the first floor — beyond an enclosed garden with flowers and a fish pond — sells Dragon Well tea, lotus root powder, liquor and other beverages, art and handicraft products.

Tianxianglou (Heavenly Fragrance Tower) Restaurant

On Jiefang (Liberation) Street in central Hangzhou beside the only remaining well of the six dug in the Tang Dynasty (618-907) for diverting drinking water from West Lake to the city, stands the Tianxiang Lou Restaurant in a three-storied Chinese-style building with six halls that can accommodate 1,200 customers at a time. First established on Jiaoren Street in 1927 with a small room large enough for only six tables, the restaurant was rebuilt at the present site after the Liberation of 1949.

On the first floor, a formal rock garden with peonies in bloom around a clear pond separates two dining halls called *"Shengyou"* (Outstanding Companions) and *"Gaopeng"* (Noble Friends). Upstairs an inscription in the handwriting of a comtemporary Hangzhou calligrapher, Guo Zhongxuan, is carved in black marble proclaiming "Heavenly Fragrance, National Flavor". Here the two dining rooms feature dishes from provinces other than Zhejiang and are named *"Qiushui"* (Autumn Lake) and *"Changtian"* (Bright Sky). These names and those of the dining halls on the first floor were taken from lines of the Tang Dynasty poet Wang Bo.

There are also two excellent dining rooms on the first floor named after two mythical islands popular in classical Chinese fiction, "Penglai" and "Yingzhou", which serve local specialties such as West Lake Vinegar Fish, Dongpo Pork, Shrimp Meat with Dragon Well Tea, Beggar's Chicken, Quick-fried Eel Slices, Immortal Chicken and Ham, Pickled Pork and Bamboo Shoots, Deep-fried Beancurd Horse's Bells, Shrimp Meat Balls, Wulin-style Roast Duck and Shrimp Roe and Winter Bamboo Shoots (see pp. 116-20 for a description of these local dishes). "Penglai" is furnished with bamboo throughout including the doors, wa!ls, tables and chairs. "Yingzhou" is furnished in a traditional Chinese style with lanterns, mahogany tables and arm-chairs.

The floor designs on all levels reflect the restaurant's name: The third floor shows ancient astronomical patterns to coincide with the first word of the restaurant's name *"tian"* or heaven, the second floor features cooking tripods to imply the second word in the restaurant's name *"xiang"* or fragrance while the first floor shows pavilions and towers to coincide with the last word of the restaurant's name "*lou*" or tower. In the open-air garden on the restaurant's roof, the Dongpo Pavilion provides a vantage point to look at the West Lake in the distance.

Zhiweiguan (Flavor Savoring Tower) Restaurant

Located at 111, Renhe Road, Zhiweiguan Restaurant is known for its variety of food, pastries and soups.

"Cat Ear" Noodle Dish is believed to have been created by a cook working at Zhiweiguan in 1913. While preparing a noodle soup with ham, chicken, dried scallops, shrimps, bamboo shoots, mushrooms and dough, he hit upon the idea of shaping the dough slices into the form of cat ears.

Besides the traditional Hangzhou specialties (see pp. 116-20) the restaurant also offers its own delicacies of fresh water products such as: Snatching the Jumping Shrimp (made with shrimp and other ingredients), Burning Monk Fahai (fresh water crab. In the story of *Lady White Snake*, when Monk Fahai, the culprit, is defeated, he hides under a crab shell), and Twin Dragons Jumping into the Sea (made with yellow croaker, mandarin fish and sea cucumbers).

The restaurant's advisory board includes Jiang Shuigen, who in the 1950s cooked West Lake Vinegar Fish for state banquets; Chen Xilin, an expert in making over 200 kinds of pastries; Zhao Aniu, known as "The King of Steamed Dumplings" and two chefs who in May 1981 traveled to the United States to cook for the Chinese Cultural and Community Center in Philadelphia.

Hangzhou Restaurant

Hangzhou Restaurant, built at the beginning of this century, serves a large range of traditional Hangzhou food. All of its dining halls spread over three stories are arranged in the traditional style of south China restaurants.

Once a restaurant famous for its wines, the Hangzhou Restaurant was described as a place where "Fragrance spread 10 *li*, inebriating its neighbors whenever a wine jug is opened." Today, its specialty is food, serving a wide variety of Hangzhou dishes prepared by first-class chefs.

Restaurant's Name	Address	Telephone
Hangzhou Restaurant	132 Yan'an Road	23477
Louwailou Restaurant	30 Wai Xi Hu (The Outer West Lake)	21654
Tianwaitian Restaurant	62 Lingyin Road	22429
Ruyizhai Restaurant	Lingyin	23001 ext.
Shanwaishan Restaurant	Yuquan (Jade Spring)	26621

Restaurant's Name	Address	Telephone
Huagang Restaurant	Huagang (Flower Harbor)	23001 ext.
Hupao Restaurant	Hupao (Tiger Spring)	23001 ext.
Jiuxi Restaurant	Jiuxi (Nine Creeks)	23001 ext.
Wushan Restaurant	Wushan (Wu Hill)	24218
Zhijian Restaurant	Liuhe Pagoda	6-421
Yuehulou Restaurant	Yuefen (Yue Fei's Tomb)	25413
Zhiweiguan Restaurant	111 Renhe Road	23655
Tianxianglou Restaurant	676 Jiefang Road	22038
Suchunzhai Restaurant	68 Yan'an Road	23235

Restaurant's Name	Address	Telephone
Tianjin Weizhen Restaurant	39 Qingnian Road	25364
Duoyichu Restaurant	23 North Zhongshan Road	21960
Wanghailou Restaurant	50 South Zhongshan Road	6-161
Ziyanglou Restaurant	388 South Zhongshan Road	26723
Tianluyuan Restaurant	35 Yuxing Street	3659
Yan'an Restaurant	88 Yan'an Road	22720
Hui Nationality Restaurant	93 Renhe Road	23860
Beijing (Peking) Restaurant	654 Qingchun Road	21658
Huibin Restaurant	Kuixiang Kou, Jiefang Road	73543
Haifeng Western Food Restaurant	169 Yan'an Road	22640
Kuiyuan Restaurant	Guanxiang Kou, Jiefang Road	25921

Local Dishes

West Lake Vinegar Fish (*Xi Hu Cu Yu* 西湖醋鱼)

A traditional dish of Hangzhou prepared with fresh grass carp. Sweet and sour.

Su Dongpo Pork (*Dong Po Rou* 东坡肉)

Braised and steamed pork, named after the poet-governor of Hangzhou.

Shrimp Meat with Dragon Well Tea (*Long Jing Xia Ren* 龙井虾仁)

Fresh water shrimps stir-fried with new tea leaves (the best, picked in early spring). Traditional specialty.

Beggar's Chicken (*Jiao Hua Tong Ji* 叫花膛鸡)

Another traditional specialty, tender chicken wrapped in lotus leaves, then paper and clay to seal in its juices while roasting.

Immortal Duck and Ham (*Huo Tong Shen Xian Ya* 火肿神仙鸭)

Duck and ham combined in a traditional Hangzhou dish.

Hibiscus Pork (*Fu Rong Rou* 芙蓉肉)

Pork tenderloin, shrimps, ham and the juice of fermented glutinous rice shaped into the form of a hibiscus.

116

Stir-fried Menhaden Fish with Spring Bamboo Shoots (*Chun Sun Chao Bu Yu* 春笋炒鲅鱼)

Popular in early spring.

Braised Shark's Fins and Ham (*Huo Tong Ba Yu Chi* 火膧扒鱼翅)

Soft fins and crisp ham in a thick broth.

Braised Bamboo Shoots with Distillers' Grains (*Zao Hui Bian Sun* 糟烩鞭笋)

Bamboo shoots prepared in the juice of distillers' grains.

Deep-fried Beancurd Horse's Bells (*Gan Zha Xiang Ling* 干炸响铃)

Pork tenderloin wrapped in a skin of soya bean milk, then deep-fried. Looks like bells on a halter.

Steamed Hilsa Herring (*Qing Zheng Shi Yu* 清蒸鲥鱼)

This fish from the Fuchun River (the middle reaches of the Qiantang River) is steamed with ham, mushrooms and bamboo shoots. Both its appealing color and taste make it one of the most popular Hangzhou dishes.

Hilsa herring, an expensive fish, is found in the coastal waters of China, Korea and the Philippines. It goes into inland rivers to breed in late spring and early summer.

"Double Happiness" Stuffed Bun (*Xing Fu Shuang* 幸福双)

Steamed cakes filled with sweetened bean paste, walnuts, dates, pine nuts and sugar — bearing the "double happiness" characters and served in pairs.

Hangzhou Rice-flour Dumplings (*Hang Zhou Tang Tuan* 杭州汤团)

A mixture of sesame or red bean paste, sugar, and sweet osmanthus wrapped up with finely ground glutinous rice. Served with soup.

Wu Hill Crisp Cakes (*Wu Shan Su You Bing* 吴山酥油饼)

Deep-fried cakes, crisp and sweet. A Hangzhou specialty.

Buns Stuffed with One Hundred Fruits (*Bai Guo You Bao* 百果油包)

Steamed dumplings filled with sweetened bean paste, walnuts, pine nuts, candied fruit, sugar and lard.

"Cat Ear" Noodle Dish (*Mao Er Duo* 猫耳朵)

Dough shaped like little cat ears is fast-boiled. Then shrimps, dried scallops, chicken, ham, and mushrooms are added to the soup.

Xi Shi's Tongue-shaped Cakes (*Xi Shi She* 西施舌)

Cakes of finely ground glutinous rice with sweet fillings, either boiled or deep-fried. Named after the ancient beauty, the cakes are also known as "Orchid Tongues".

Round Dumplings Steamed on Pine Needles (*Song Si Tang Bao* 松丝汤包)

Dumplings made of wheat flour with pork filling are steamed on a bed of pine needles in a steamer so that they have the fragrance of pine. Served with an egg soup.

West Lake Watershield Soup (*Xi Hu Chun Cai Tang* 西湖莼菜汤)

Watershield, grown at Three Pools Mirroring the Moon and Viewing Fish at Flower Harbor, is a Hangzhou specialty — the edible leaves of an aquatic plant harvested from mid-April until the end of September and made into a soup. Said to be rich in vitamin C with the medicinal value of stopping nausea and soothing ulcers.

Other Dishes:

Home-made Salted Pork (*Jia Xiang Nan Rou* 家乡南肉)

Fish-head Broth (*Yu Tou Nong Tang* 鱼头浓汤)

As-Good-As-Crab-Meat Thick Broth (*Sai Xie Geng* 赛蟹羹)

Quick-fried Prawns (*You Bao Da Xia* 油爆大虾)

Home-made Salted Pork with Spring Bamboo Shoots (*Nan Rou Chun Sun* 南肉春笋)

Stewed Fish-head with Beancurd (*Yu Tou Dou Fu* 鱼头豆腐)

Quick-fried Eel Slices (*Sheng Bao Shan Pian* 生爆鳝片)

Quick-boiled Crucian Carp with Clam (*Ha Li Cuan Ji Yu* 蛤蜊汆鲫鱼)

Stir-fried Spring Chicken with Chestnuts (*Li Zi Chao Zi Ji* 栗子炒子鸡)

Duck with Boiled Dumplings (*Shui Jiao Ya Zi* 水饺鸭子)

Steamed Pork with Rice Flour in Lotus Leaf (*He Ye Fen Zheng Rou* 荷叶粉蒸肉)

Fish Meat Balls (*Zhan Yu Wan* 斩鱼丸)

Rice Crusts with Shrimp Meat and Tomato Sauce (*Fan Qie Xia Ren Guo Ba* 蕃茄虾仁锅巴)

Hangzhou Soya-sauce Duck (*Hang Zhou Jiang Ya* 杭州酱鸭)

"Eight-treasure" Spring Chicken (*Ba Bao Tong Ji* 八宝童鸡)

Chestnuts Fried with Winter Mushrooms (*Li Zi Chao Dong Gu* 栗子炒冬菇)

Shrimp Roe and Winter Bamboo Shoots (*Xia Zi Dong Sun* 虾子冬笋)

Steamed Glutinous Rice with "Eight-treasures" (*Zhu You Ba Bao Fan* 猪油八宝饭)

Noodles in Soup with Pork Slices and Bamboo Shoots (*Pian Er Chuan Mian* 片儿川面)

"Eight-treasure" Glutinous Rice Steamed in Lotus Leaf (*He Ye Ba Bao Fan* 荷叶八宝饭)

Fried Noodles with Winter Mushrooms (*Dong Gu Chao Mian* 冬菇炒面)

Chestnut Thick Soup with Sweet Osmanthus Flowers (*Gui Hua Xian Li Geng* 桂花鲜栗羹)

Noodles with Quick-fried Eel Shreds and Shelled Shrimps (*Xia Bao Shan Mian* 虾爆鳝面)

Hotels and Guesthouses

The hotels listed below include rooms with bath, air-conditioning, heat, service attendants who speak some English and — if desired — Western-style breakfast. At peak seasons, some non-Chinese foreign visitors may find themselves housed at the Overseas Chinese Hotel, which is convenient to both town and the lake area, but where most attendants do not speak English. Most hotels also have a dormitory space available at student rates. In a class by itself is the Xihu Guesthouse, opened in 1979 for

foreign tourists, which has always been used to accommodate high state officials — it was a favorite of visiting heads of state like Yugoslavia's Marshal Josip Tito, former U.S. President Richard Nixon and Spain's King Juan Carlos. The guest residence is directly under the management of the provincial government. The price for a room in the guesthouse complex of four main buildings, based on the design of the original villa and gardens built by a Qing Dynasty official in 1879, varies from the average cost for any accommodations for foreigners in Hangzhou to 100 times that for a suite in luxurious Building One. Guests may stroll around the 300,000-square-meter garden — considered one of the finest in Hangzhou — with its small bridges and ornamental rocks to listen to the orioles, enjoy watching the ducks fly off the lake from one of the waterside pavilions, and smell the fragrance of the osmanthus flowers. Except for the railing on the stone bridge at the entrance, little survives from the original villa. The garden includes a stele inscribed by Wu Changshuo, the Qing Dynasty painter and founder of the Xiling Seal-Engraving Society.

Name	Location	Telephone	Facilities
Hangzhou Hotel	Beishan Rd. (North of the lake)	22921	Dining room, hairdresser's, shop, bank, post & telegraph office, telex (sending only), café, CITS ticket agency, taxi.
Xiling Guesthouse	Beishan Rd. (North of the lake)	22921	

Name	Location	Tele-phone	Facilities
Huagang Hotel	Xishan Rd. (West of the lake	71324	Dining room, hairdresser's, shop, café, separate dining room featuring local specialties.
Huajiashan Guesthouse	Santaishan	71224	Dining room, hairdresser's, shop.
Zhejiang Guesthouse	Santaishan	24483	Dining room, hairdresser's, shop, indoor swimming pool.
Huaqiao Hotel (Overseas Chinese Hotel)	Hubin Rd. (Near the city)	23401	Dining room, hairdresser's, shop, taxi, clinic.
Xihu Guesthouse	Lakeside	24068	Dining room, hairdresser's.
Dahua Hotel	Nanshan Rd. (South of the lake)	23901	Dining room, hairdresser's, shop.
Xinxin Hotel	Beishan Rd. (North of the lake)	24074	Dining room.

Theaters and Cinemas

Performances of "southern-style" traditional Chinese operas which originated in Zhejiang Province are frequently given by the several resident opera companies in Hangzhou: the first and second Zhejiang Yue Opera troupes and the Hangzhou Yue Opera Troupe, the Zhejiang Shao Opera Troupe, the Kun Opera Troupe and the Zhejiang Peking Opera Troupe. Their repertoires include hundreds of operas (some of which take over three hours to perform) such as *Recognizing Mother at the Nunnery*, *Monkey King Thrice Strikes the White-bone Demon*, *The Monk and Nun's Tryst*, and *Peach Blossom Fan*.

Performances are also frequently presented by the Zhejiang Modern Drama Troupe, the Zhejiang Song and Dance Ensemble, the Zhejiang Folk Art Ensemble, the Hangzhou Modern Drama Troupe, the Hangzhou Folk Art Group and the Hangzhou Acrobatic Troupe.

The two morning papers, the *Zhejiang Daily* and the *Hangzhou Daily*, list the current goings-on at the theaters and cinemas in town.

Name	Address	Telephone
Hangzhou Theater	Tiyuchang Road	26608
Great Hall of the People	Yan'an Road	25988

Name	Address	Telephone
Zhejiang Victory Theater	Yan'an Road	21761
Dongpo Theater	Dongpo Road	23966
New China Theater	Qingnian Road	22585
Red Star Theater	Jianguonan Road	23540
Gongshu Theater	Chatingmiao	3023
The Pacific Cinema	Jiefang Road	24365
New China Cinema	Guohuo Street	25254
West Lake Cinema	Pinghai Street	25548
The People's Cinema	Jianguobei Road	72846
Qianjin Cinema	Houshi Street	21635
Guangming Cinema	Nanxing Bridge	21968
Dazhong Cinema	Yuxing Street	3620
Hangzhou Workers' Cultural Palace	Renhe Road	24630

Tourism and Travel

Chinese tourists come to Hangzhou in all seasons to see the sights and to watch such special events as the West Lake Lantern Festival and the West Lake Boat Race. Buddhist holidays also bring large numbers to Hangzhou, especially to Temple of the Soul's Retreat where an estimated 100,000 come each year to celebrate Buddha's birthday on the eighth day of the fourth lunar month (usually around mid-May). Hangzhou is always popular with honeymooners.

Foreign tourists began coming in increasing numbers in the late 1970s. Some 40,000 foreign tourists visited Hangzhou in 1980. This number increased in 1981 to 55,000 people from 84 countries with the most coming from Japan, and next the United States. The Hangzhou branch office of the China International Travel Service points out that this number includes only tourists handled by CITS and not students, handled by the education departments and youth organizations; businessmen, sponsored by foreign trade agencies; or people who are in the country on individual visas.

According to CITS, foreign tourists are people who come from all walks of life whose special needs and interests the organization tries to accommodate.

"For instance," said Yuan Ruinan, Deputy Manager of CITS, Hangzhou Branch, "some educators would rather spend their time visiting schools and give up sightseeing."

Besides Zhejiang University, an institution of higher

learning specializing in science and technology which boasts a Nobel Prize winner, Tsung-dao Lee, among its former students, and Hangzhou University, there are numerous technical secondary schools and specialized institutes of higher learning like the Silk Industry Institute in Hangzhou.

Doctors are also taken at their request to visit the many sanitoria in the nearby hills for people with chronic, non-infectious diseases as well as resort villas for model workers who have earned a vacation. Another place of interest to visitors from the medical profession is the Hangzhou No. 2 Traditional Chinese Pharmaceutical Works in the northwest suburbs where modern techniques are used to extract herbs for injections.

Tours with interpreters are also available to silk factories, communes, hospitals and industries. There are quite a number of good hikes to take — both in the hills and around the lake.

The weather in Hangzhou's sub-tropical, monsoon climate is changeable and generally warm, humid and rainy. It is hot in summer and can snow in winter. Spring — a time of frequent rain — is generally considered the best time to visit for the flowers though the osmanthus blooms in autumn and the plum blooms in winter.

The amount of time foreign tourists spend in Hangzhou varies but, typically, Hangzhou is included among five or six cities in a two-week CITS tour of China, which means a stay of two to three days for the "average" tourist.

Travel to Hangzhou

Hangzhou is easily accessible by both air and rail. Frequent flights are scheduled by the Civil Aviation

ROUTE MAP

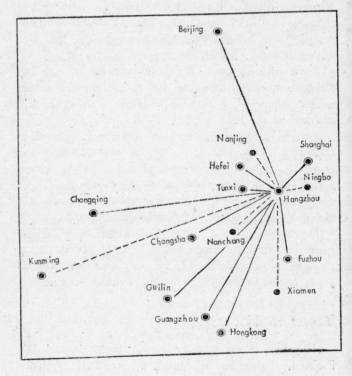

Either by air or by train
------ Only by train

Beijing

Nanjing   Shanghai

Hefei   Ningbo

Tunxi   Hangzhou

Chongqing

Changsha Nanchang

Kunming   Fuzhou

Guilin   Xiamen

Guangzhou

Hongkong

Administration of China (CAAC) between Hangzhou and Beijing, Shanghai, Hefei, Tunxi, Guangzhou, Fuzhou, Changsha, Guilin and Hongkong. One of the centers of railway travel in southeastern China, Hangzhou is at the end of the Beijing-Hangzhou Railway and the departure point for the Hangzhou-Nanchang, Hangzhou-Ningbo and Hangzhou-Changsha railways. Shanghai is about three hours away by train. Highways also extend in all directions.

Travel in Hangzhou

Most scenic spots are accessible by Hangzhou's excellent public bus system. The No. 7 running between the Hangzhou Railway Station and the Temple of the Soul's Retreat, for example, sends buses once every three minutes or so until 9:45 p.m. from the railway station to travel along the Bai Causeway to Solitary Hill Island, over Xiling Bridge and past the Hangzhou Hotel, Yue Fei's Tomb and Temple, Jade Spring and the Hangzhou Botanical Gardens to the temple. The first bus on the return trip leaves the Temple of the Soul's Retreat at 5:30 a.m. and service continues until 9 p.m. The following is a list of the 36 bus routes and four trolley routes in Hangzhou:

Public Bus Service:

No. 1. Hangzhou Cotton Mill — Pinghai Street
2. Nanxing Bridge — Six Harmonies Pagoda
3. Wulin Gate — Nanxing Bridge
4. Yan'an Road — Nine Creeks
5. Kuixiang (Sunflower Lane) — Ding Bridge

5. (Feeder line) Yan'an Road — Shiqiao (Stone Bridge)
6. Wulin Gate — Yuhang County
7. Railway Station — Lingyin (Temple of the Soul's Retreat)
8. Genshan Gate — Meihuabei (Plum Stela)
9. Kuixiang (Sunflower Lane) — Linping Town
10. Hubin (Lakeside) — The Silk College
11. Songmuchang — Railway Station
12. Genshan Electric Station — Liuwencun Village
13. Wulin Gate — Pingyao Town
13. (Feeder line) Wulin Gate — Sandun
14. Nine Creeks — Fuyang County
15. Yan'an Road — Xiaoshan County
16. Hubin (Lakeside) — Zhejiang University
17. Genshan Gate — Kang Bridge
18. Nine Creeks — Yuanpu
19. Linping Town — Tangqi Town
20. Qianjiang River — Hongken Farm
21. Linping Town — Hangbo (Hangzhou Glass Factory)
22. Nanxing Bridge — Wenjiayan
23. Kuixiang (Sunflower Lane) — Yuanjiaba
24. Yan'an Road — Meijiawu
25. Kuixiang (Sunflower Lane) — Qibao Town
26. Zhaohui Xincun — Huimin Road
27. Pinghai Street — Dragon Well Production Brigade
29. Gongchen Bridge — Hangbo (Hangzhou Glass Factory)
31. Liuxia Town — Zhuantang

32. Hangbo (Hangzhou Glass Factory) — Tangqi Town
34. Nine Creeks — Zhoupu

Special Touring Bus Lines:

- Hangzhou Zoo — Longjing Teahouse
- Temple of the Soul's Retreat — Hangzhou Zoo
- Hubin (Lakeside) — Foot of Jade Emperor Hill

Trolleys:

No. 51 Gongchen Bridge — Railway Station
52 Wulin Gate — Nanxing Bridge
53 Wulin Gate — Railway Station
54 (Circling Line) Genshan Electric Station — Wulin Gate — Genshan Electric Station

Taxis can be hired at any hotel. Motorized pedicabs are also available at the railway station, by the Lakeside Park and at Wulin Gate.

Travel to Nearby Places

Shaoxing

At the foot of Xiling Bridge in Hangzhou stands a white marble statue erected in 1981 designed by the Zhejiang Fine Arts Institute of Qiu Jin, the woman revolutionary who was beheaded by the Qing government in 1907. Across the island, another new monument is being built in memory of Lu Xun, the revolutionary writer who died in 1936. The birthplace of both these historic figures is claimed by Shaoxing, only an hour's train ride from Hangzhou across fields planted with bamboo, wheat, barley, rice, cotton and sweet potatoes. A trip to the canal town Shaoxing for its scenic sites alone would be worth it with its East Lake (*Dong Hu*), the magnificent Temple of Great Yu (*Dayu Ling*) built in the 6th century and the Orchid Pavilion (*Lan Ting*) where China's most distinguished calligrapher of the 4th century Wang Xizhi wrote and composed poems. Visitors here will have a chance to see a typical south China landscape rich in rivers and lakes — canoes covered with bamboo awnings shuttle along the criss-crossing waterways and numerous lakes and ponds that stud the vast area of the Shaoxing plain. Shaoxing's rice wine is one of China's most celebrated. Other local products that are in high demand on both domestic and foreign markets include Pingshui gunpowder tea, paper fans, silk, felt hats, porcelain and inkstone. But as more Western visitors with a growing sophistication about modern China arrive, it may be the home of Qiu Jin and the home and Memorial Hall of Lu Xun that offer the deepest attraction.

"It's reading Lu Xun that has helped me most to understand China," said Steve Chapman, a 27-year-old graduate of St. Olaf's College in Minnesota in Chinese studies. An American business representative of Pillsbury's Green Giant Products, Chapman was visiting Hangzhou in January 1982 with his wife, Cindy, to help administer his company's compensation trade agreement with the Hangzhou Canned Food Factory, one of the largest of its kind in China.

This kind of respect for the man many regard as China's greatest 20th century writer brings visitors to Shaoxing just because it is Lu Xun's birthplace. Among foreign tourists, this has especially included visitors from Japan where Lu Xun studied from 1902 to 1909.

Originally enrolled in medical school in Sendai in Japan, Lu Xun abandoned medicine for literature after viewing a newsreel slide of a Chinese being beheaded by the Japanese during the Russo-Japanese War while other Chinese looked on apathetically. ". . . This slide convinced me that medical science was not so important after all. The people of a weak and backward country, however strong and healthy they might be, could only serve to be made examples of or as witnesses of such futile spectacles; and it was not necessarily deplorable if many of them died of illness. The most important thing, therefore, is to change their spirit; and since at that time I felt that literature was the best means to this end, I decided to promote a literary movement."[1]

From then on, he dedicated his life to opposing feudalism and imperialism through writing, founding literary groups and magazines, and supporting other revolutionary writers and activists. One of his best known works, *The True Story of Ah Q*, points out the failure of the Revolution of 1911 led by the bourgeoisie. He taught literature at Beijing University and other universities and served as dean and head of the literature department at Sun Yat-sen University in Guangzhou. A classical Chinese scholar, he pioneered in writing essays in the vernacular and translated over 200 literary works by over 100 writers from 14 countries "to borrow fire from other countries to light up the dark night in China". Frequently forced to move to avoid arrest throughout his life, often under cover, he died of tuberculosis in Shanghai in 1936.

The Memorial Hall of Lu Xun — not far from Shaoxing Middle School where he taught science upon his return from Japan — takes visitors past displays organized in chronological order around a central courtyard of books, personal items and photographs relating to the people and events in Lu Xun's life. Among the items on sale at the memorial hall's shop is a handsome batik cloth calligraphy of his poem: "Fierce-browed, I coolly defy a thousand pointing fingers; Head-bowed, like a willing ox I serve the children."

Next door to the memorial hall is Lu Xun's family home, made a museum in 1953, which is furnished with original family furniture and household items such as the sewing basket, iron and scissors used by his mother. Following through the living quarters where Lu Xun is said to have met with close friends and students during the Revolution

---

[1] Lu Xun, *Selected Works, op. cit.*, Volume I, pp. 12-13.

of 1911, the garden is reached which Lu Xun described in his essay "From Hundred-Plant Garden to Three-Flavor Study" as his childhood "paradise" where he came to catch crickets and to try to catch birds. The original garden wall described in the essay still stands.

"A few hundred yards east of our house, across a stone bridge, was where my teacher lived," Lu Xun wrote. "You went in through a black-lacquered bamboo gate, and the third room was the classroom. On the central wall hung the inscription Three-Flavor Study, and under this was a painting of a portly fallow deer lying beneath an old tree. In the absence of a tablet to Confucius, we bowed before the inscription and the deer. The first time for Confucius, the second time for our teacher."[1]

Today the walk from the garden to where Lu Xun began his studies at the age of 12 is just as he described it. Lu Xun's desk is in the back right-hand corner from the scroll. The character for "early" is carved into the desk by Lu Xun after he was once reprimanded by his teacher for being late. The plum tree in the garden described by Lu Xun in the essay still stands while the two osmanthus trees are more recent additions.

About a ten-minute drive across town is the home of Qiu Jin (1877-1907), also preserved as a museum, which reflects the standing of her bureaucrat-landlord family in its series of rooms — now filled with display cases and photographs — connected by corridors. Immediately to the right of the main hall is her bedroom with her desk and bed which is pulled back from its original position to show the opening of a hidden inner room where she stored weapons. The scrolls hanging on the wall are inscribed

---

[1] Lu Xun, *Selected Works, op. cit.,* Volume I, p. 392.

with characters which add up to one word: study. The displays arranged throughout the rest of the house document her life which included a brief marriage forced on her by her family to a man with opposing views.

Qiu Jin also went to study in Japan where in the autumn of 1904 she started a newspaper in Tokyo advocating Chinese revolution and women's rights. In July 1905, she met with Dr. Sun Yat-sen after his arrival in Tokyo to organize the China Revolutionary League and was recommended to become the league's organizer in Zhejiang Province.

Returning to China, Qiu Jin established the *Chinese Women's Journal* in which she wrote in its first issue: "Now I want to unite a group of 200 million people ... so China's women can gain a new lease on life, unleash their energies and forge ahead to hasten the dawn of a golden age."

Under the pen-name, "The Chivalrous Woman of Jianhu Lake,"[1] Qiu Jin also wrote poetry, including this one with a West Lake allusion, "Plums": "Thousands of trees on Solitary Hill brave the winter frost/I am one of their sprigs."

The museum displays several photographs of Qiu Jin, including perhaps the best known of her taken in Japan in which she is dressed in kimono and holds a sword in her hand. She is second to the left in the top row of the picture of members of a women's group dedicated to revolution. Other photographs show her in men's clothes which she often wore after joining the revolution. Among the displays under glass are her shawl and her sword.

---

[1] Jianhu Lake is now used as another name for Shaoxing. The actual lake is located about two kilometers southwest of the town. The famous Shaoxing rice wine is made from the lake water.

Qiu Jin went on to become the headmaster of Datong School in Shaoxing which, as a revolutionary center, was surrounded on July 13, 1907 by Qing troops. Arrested during the struggle, Qiu Jin reportedly told her captors under torture: "You ought not to ask so many questions about the activities of the Revolutionary Party." On the wall of the museum hangs a painting showing her written response to her captors' request for a confession: "Autumn rain, autumn wind, I grieve."

On July 15, 1907 she was beheaded at Xuantingkou in Shaoxing County. In 1908 some of her close friends buried her remains near Xiling Bridge near West Lake. They were later removed to Hunan Province but after the Revolution of 1911 were once again disinterred and buried on the banks of West Lake where a marker rests beside her statue. A monument to Qiu Jin was also erected in the center of Shaoxing. On a visit to the town in 1939, the late Premier Zhou Enlai whose family was a'so from Shaoxing wrote a poem, also in the Qiu Jin museum, to his cousin encouraging her to learn from Qiu Jin: "Don't forget the spirit of the Chivalrous Woman of Jianhu Lake".

Xin'an River Hydroelectric Power Station

The Xin'an River Hydroelectric Power Station, which is the first major water electricity generating plant built by the Chinese with a capacity of some 650,000 kw, is about 160 kilometers from Hangzhou. The plant stands in an area appreciated for its scenic beauty, particularly the huge lake which feeds the plant. Under normal circumstances, the water area is 580 square kilometers. Numerous islands, 17 of which are 0.5 square kilometers in area each and 300 a little under 0.5 square kilometers each, stud the lake, earning it the name "The Lake of a Thousand Islands".

Xin'an River (which is the upper reaches of the same river of which the Qiantang River makes up the lower reaches) attracts people with its grotesque cliffs, caves, mountains and waterfalls as well as sites of historical interest. The source of the river is Mount Huangshan, also a well-known scenic spot, in Anhui Province northwest of Zhejiang. A new tourist route — Hangzhou-Xin'an River-Mount Huangshan — is expected to be opened soon which will cover some of China's best-known lakes, rivers and mountains.

Mount Mogan

A summer resort about 82 kilometers from Hangzhou by highway built in the early 20th century with Western-style hotels, villas, tennis courts and swimming pools. The area is famous for its natural springs and waterfalls and bamboo forests.

Grand Canal

One of the engineering wonders of ancient China, the Grand Canal was built in the Sui Dynasty to link Beijing with Hangzhou, its southern terminus. Vestiges of the original canal remain, and parts of the canal are navigable. CITS sends tour buses to Huzhou where boats are then taken up the canal along Taihu Lake to the city of Wuxi, about 190 kilometers from Hangzhou.

Yaolin Wonderland

A cave in Tonglu County, 85 kilometers northeast of Hangzhou, this place began to attract visitors as early as the Sui and Tang dynasties (581-907) but was buried in oblivion for a long time until it was rediscovered in 1979 by a scientific expedition. One kilometer in depth, the limestone cave includes stalactites, stalagmites, peaks and rocks of unusual colors and shapes, streams, pools and canyons in six "halls" interconnected with passages and chambers. The cave covers an area of 28,000 square meters with a ceiling which goes up 30 meters at its highest point.

Ningbo

This east coast port city 168 kilometers from Hangzhou traces its history as the capital of Yue back to the 770-475 B.C. in the Spring and Autumn Period. It became one of the country's ports for foreign trade in the Tang Dynasty and one of the five "treaty ports" opened to foreign countries following the Opium War. Ningbo attracts visitors with its beautiful seaside scenery, historical relics, sites of historical interest, and local handicrafts and food.

Putuo Island

Putuo Island, one of the major Buddhist centers in China since antiquity, is also known for its scenic beauty — all contained on a narrow 12.5-square-kilometer island in the East China Sea of the easternmost end of the Zhoushan Archipelago off the mainland of Zhejiang Province. The island is 50 nautical miles from Ningbo. Recently re-opened to foreign visitors, Putuo Island with Jinhua, Emei and Wutai mountains is regarded as one of the four holiest Buddhist mountains in China. Amid its green woods are over a hundred Buddhist monasteries, nunneries and other shrines. The three biggest monasteries — Puji, Fayu and Huiji — are admired for their magnificent architecture and rich golden colors. Other treasures housed on the island include paintings of the Tang Dynasty (618-907), Yuan (1271-1368) pagodas, Ming (1368-1644) carvings, Buddhist statues from Tibet, and art objects from Southeast Asian countries.

The scenic beauty of the island includes grotesque rocks, green cypress and pine, twisting caves, clear springs and ancient trees. A good place to go swimming is along the 1.5 kilometers of Thousand-Pace Beach (*Qianbu Sha*) and the Hundred-Pace Beach (*Baibu Sha*). Other notable scenic spots include the Tide Sound Cave (*Chaoyin Dong*), Pantuo Rock (*Pantuo Shi*), Lotus Pool (*Lian Chi*) and Buddha Statue Peak (*Foding Shan*).

Tiantai Hill

Some 223 kilometers southeast of Hangzhou in Zhejiang Province's Tiantai County is Tiantai Hill, known as the birthplace of the Tiantai Sect of Chinese Buddhism. The

Guoqing Temple here, built in the Sui Dynasty (581-618), includes 14 temple halls with over 600 rooms. Since the temple has had close historic links with Buddhism in Japan, it is especially popular with Japanese visitors.

Three kilometers to the north of Tiantai County, stands a gem of ancient Chinese architecture — a 1,300-year-old hexagonal pagoda of the Sui Dynasty which is seven meters in height with two stories.

Grand Buddha Temple (*Dafo Si*)

Some 165 kilometers away from Hangzhou on the way to Guoqing Temple in Tiantai County is the Grand Buddha Temple. Built against the cliffs of Nanming Hill is an exquisite 13.23-meter-high Maitreya Buddha statue carved on the cliff, sitting cross-legged with hands placed on the lap, palms upward. The statue is so huge that one palm can hold over a dozen people. Work on the statue began in 486 and was completed in 516.

Yandang Mountains

Some 392 kilometers away from Hangzhou the Wild Goose and Reed Marsh (*Yandang*) Mountains in Leqing County, southern Zhejiang Province, have attracted visitors for centuries with their dramatic peaks, caves, rocks and waterfalls.

The Yandang Mountains have some peaks rising straight from the ground into the clouds. Other peaks offer different images when looked at from different angles while waterfalls tumble down their sides from high sheer cliffs.

One of several hundred scenic spots in the area, the lake at Wild Goose and Reed Marsh Ridge (*Yandang Gang*) on the main peak gives the place its name by attracting wild geese in the autumn with its reeds and grass.

The Wild Goose and Reed Marsh Mountains, covering 450 square kilometers, are divided into seven scenic zones with Spirits Peak (*Ling Feng*), Spirits Crag (*Ling Yan*) and Great Dragon Pool (*Dalong Qiu*) including the most attractions. The other zones are Wild Goose Lake (*Yan Hu*), Victory Manifestation Gate (*Xiansheng Men*), Fairy Bridge (*Xian Qiao*) and Goat Horn Cave (*Yangjiao Dong*).

Mt. Mogao

Hongniao

Mt. Liuqingzh

Yaojino
Wonderland

Xia Yichun River

TO CHANGZHOU

Hangzhou Monthly Temperatures (F)

Temperature (Approx) Month	Average	Low	High
Jan.	38.84	33	46.58
Feb.	41	35	48.92
March	48.74	42	56.84
April	59.36	52	68
May	68.36	62	76.64
June	75.56	70	84.48
July	83.48	77	92.12
Aug.	82.58	76	91.22
Sep.	74.3	69	82.22
Oct.	63.5	56	72.5
Nov.	53.78	47	62.78
Dec.	42.98	37	52

Suggested Tours

These are only suggestions — one way to get in most of the major sites in a three-day visit. Certainly many other combinations are possible, and some visitors may prefer to sacrifice seeing a number of sites for spending a more leisurely time at a few. Either Temple of the Soul's Retreat or Yue Fei's Tomb and Temple, for example, could take a full half-day in itself.

First Day,

Morning: A boat ride on West Lake followed by visits to Three Pools Mirroring the Moon, Flower Harbor Park, and Six Harmonies Pagoda.

Afternoon: Temple of the Soul's Retreat, Jade Spring, Hangzhou Botanical Gardens and Yue Fei's Tomb and Temple.

Second Day,

Morning: Hangzhou Silk and Brocade Factory (or a visit to some other industry, school or one of the other silk factories), Wu Hill and downtown.

Afternoon: Sun Yat-sen Park, Xiling Seal-Engraving Society, Autumn Moon on Calm Lake and Baochu Pagoda.

Third Day,

Morning: Meijiawu Village, Dragon Well, Hangzhou Flower Nursery and Yellow Dragon Cave.

Afternoon: Tiger Spring, Hangzhou Zoo and Three Caves at Yanxia.

Index

145

西 湖 揽 胜

莎拉·格拉姆斯 著

*

浙江人民出版社
外文出版社出版
（中国北京百万庄路24号）
外文印刷厂印刷
中国国际书店发行
（北京399信箱）
1983年（24开）第一版
编号：（英）12050—66
00150
12—E—1596PA

Tourist Map of Hangzhou

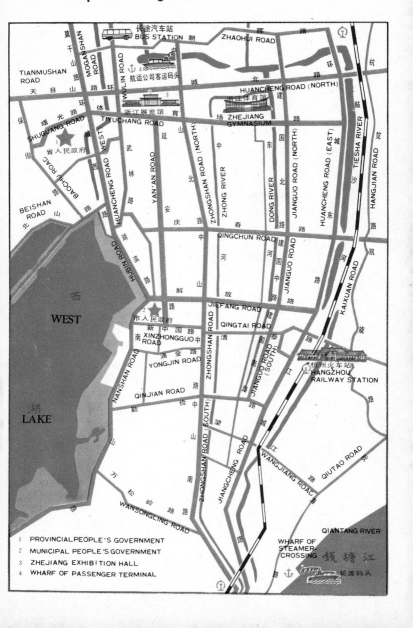